Don Sisk
Ps. 126:5.6

THE LIFE STORY OF
DON SISK
WHERE ONLY GOD COULD LEAD

CARY SCHMIDT

FOREWORD BY PAUL CHAPPELL

Copyright © 2015 by Striving Together Publications. All Scripture quotations are taken from the King James Version. Special emphasis in verses is added.

First published in 2015 by Striving Together Publications, a ministry of Lancaster Baptist Church, Lancaster, CA 93535. Striving Together Publications is committed to providing tried, trusted, and proven books that will further equip local churches to carry out the Great Commission. Your comments and suggestions are valued.

All rights reserved. No part of this book may be reproduced, stored in a retrieval system, or transmitted in any form or by any means—electronic, mechanical, photocopy, recording, or otherwise—without written permission of the publisher, except for brief quotations in printed reviews.

Striving Together Publications
4020 E. Lancaster Blvd.
Lancaster, CA 93535
800.201.7748

Cover design by Andrew Jones
Cover photo by Daniel Straub
Layout by Craig Parker
Edited by Sonia Birdsong
Special thanks to our proofreaders

The author and publication team have given every effort to give proper credit to quotes and thoughts that are not original with the author. It is not our intent to claim originality with any quote or thought that could not readily be tied to an original source.

ISBN 978-1-59894-289-7
Printed in the United States of America

CONTENTS

Introduction v

One—The Lord Gave 1
Two—The Lord Protected 9
Three—The Lord Saved 19
Four—The Lord Taught 31
Five—The Lord Answered 39
Six—The Lord Called 47
Seven—The Lord Developed 61
Eight—The Lord Prepared 71
Nine—The Lord Humbled 83
Ten—The Lord Renewed 101
Eleven—The Lord Stretched 109
Twelve—The Lord Enlarged 119
Thirteen—The Lord Disrupted 127
Fourteen—The Lord Sustained 135
Fifteen—The Lord Directed 145
Sixteen—The Lord Expanded 153
Seventeen—The Lord Surprised 161
Eighteen—The Lord Provided 173
Nineteen—The Lord Redirected 181
Twenty—The Lord Preserved 187

Conclusion—The Lord Led 193

Foreword

Of all the places the Lord has led Dr. Don Sisk, I will be eternally thankful that a pastor's fellowship in Atlanta, Georgia, some twenty-five years ago was among them.

I'll never forget that day. In God's providence, Dr. Sisk and I both attended that meeting. The meeting turned out to be non-edifying and issue-orientated, and before it was over, I found myself seated on the back row in a session, wondering why I had even come. Minutes later, a white-haired man with a big smile sat down next to me and introduced himself as Don Sisk. Learning I was a pastor, he gave me his recent book, *Joyful Giving*.

Dr. Sisk and I look back on that meeting and chuckle. During the meeting, we both (separately) wondered why we had come. Today, both of us realize that God led us there for the very simple reason of meeting each other.

Over the years, Dr. Sisk has become one of my dearest friends and most-trusted mentors. He loves the Lord, loves God's people, and loves the lost like no other man I know.

You can't be around Dr. Sisk long without catching his passion for the Great Commission and his heart for the needy harvest fields around the world. Not only did he plant two churches in Japan, but God has also used him greatly to stir churches in the States for worldwide evangelism. At the time I met Dr. Sisk, Lancaster Baptist Church supported two missionaries with just over $2,000 per year going to missions. Since that time, and with Dr. Sisk's help, we've been able to add over 220 missionaries and give over $1,000,000 annually to missions.

For the past almost fifteen years, Dr. Sisk has served as the head of our missions department here at West Coast Baptist College, which means he is here in Lancaster several months a year. This is an obvious benefit to our students, but it's a tremendous benefit to me as well. His office is just across the hallway from mine, and each time he arrives, I look forward to visiting with him and receiving his counsel.

Don and Virginia Sisk have labored tirelessly to encourage and bless my family, teach and counsel our college students, and serve literally thousands of God's servants around the world.

I've seen Dr. Sisk when he was not treated well by others respond with kindness and grace. I've seen him when he was not feeling well extend himself to serve others. I've seen him when he was in the midst of tremendous personal trials radiate the joy of the Lord.

Dr. Sisk is to me an example of personal, financial, and spiritual integrity. He's a man who walks in holiness and gives grace. He loves his wife (to whom he's been married for sixty-three years), and he loves God's work (which he's labored in for sixty years). His testimony is one of faithfulness, diligence, kindness, and tremendous fruit in every place God has allowed him to serve, which now includes the entire world.

I'm thrilled that Dr. Sisk's story is now in print. I'm excited for you to be holding it in your hands. In these pages, you'll find a record of the faithful leading of God in the life of His servant. You'll be encouraged to follow God's leading in your life, and you'll be challenged to invest your life in ways that make an eternal difference.

Paul Chappell
Pastor, Lancaster Baptist Church
Lancaster, California

Introduction

Anyone who has been privileged to know them will agree there have never been two more delightful people than Don and Virginia Sisk. They embody so many valuable, biblical qualities, and they exemplify Christian joy and grace as authentically as I have ever witnessed. And there are few people alive that have genuinely impacted more souls on so many continents with the gospel of Christ—either directly through personal soulwinning and church planting or indirectly through preaching and mentoring and assisting missionaries around the world.

Often, when I see Dr. Sisk, I'll smile and say, "Well, there he is! The father of modern missions!" But the Lord knows, I've never meant it jokingly. God has used Don Sisk to impact New Testament missions around the world more than any other person I know today. Recently when preaching, in an "off the cuff" comment, he estimated that over one hundred million dollars has been given to missions through conferences he has preached in during his ministry. The statement slipped by so quickly and was spoken in such a humble manner that probably few people caught it. He wasn't bragging; he wasn't taking the credit. He was simply glorifying God and encouraging the church family at Lancaster Baptist Church that many churches around the world are doing as they are—generously giving to support missions. But the statement struck me deeply.

Obviously, in each conference where Dr. Sisk has preached, God used many contributing factors to lead a church family to give—the pastor, the music, the preaching, the needs, and, most importantly, the Holy Spirit of God using the grace of God to compel people to give. But when it comes to missions giving and young people's surrendering to God's call to go, God has anointed and blessed the sacrificial ministry of Dr. Don Sisk like few others. He has been a tool in God's hands to compel many to the field or to a more generous support of global evangelization.

Nine years ago, I began to speak with Dr. Don Sisk and Dr. Paul Chappell about the possibility of developing a biography about Don Sisk. At first Dr. Sisk chuckled at the thought—as if to say, "Who would want to read it?" But after some prodding and some thought, he agreed to the idea—hoping that his story might encourage and help others to give their lives in full surrender and service to the Lord.

Over a twenty-four month period, Dr. Sisk spent countless hours dictating the details and events of his life and drawing stories and principles from many of his sermons over the years. In compiling this information, the Lord has placed several priorities on my heart. This is my prayer for the chapters that follow:

To glorify God—Don Sisk is a living sacrifice to his Lord and Saviour, Jesus Christ. I pray these pages will bring the same glory to the Lord that Dr. Sisk's life does.

To accurately tell the compelling story of a great life—I want the facts to be not only correct, but also to tell a story as captivating as the heart of the man they chronicle.

INTRODUCTION

To convey the true personality and authenticity of Don Sisk—He loves to laugh, and I hope this manuscript will bring you laughter. He loves his Saviour, and I pray you will too, even more after reading. He somehow finds the delicate balance between living soberly and righteously but also expressing joy and delight with every aspect of life.

To draw upon the practical biblical principles that are embodied in this well-lived life—Don Sisk is a living example of what a joyful Christian should be. I pray the Lord will challenge you with the biblical principles that form this man's foundation.

To show the sovereign hand of God in every context and season of Don Sisk's life—We all tend to lose sight of God's hand in the daily details of our lives. At eighty-two years of age, Dr. Sisk looks back and sees God's hand in every season quite clearly. May these pages remind you that God is at work in your life even when you can't see Him. Someday, if you stay faithful to Him, you will look back and see His leading with crystal clarity.

Don Sisk loves life, he loves people, and he loves the Lord. In the following pages, I invite you to share in the story of the life of a modern-day spiritual hero. May his life compel you to surrender and serve the Saviour who died for you, and may you run your race with the same joyful commitment.

One

THE LORD GAVE

2006

Summer was drawing to a close, but the brisk memories of palatial, Alaskan glaciers were still fresh in the minds of Don and Virginia Sisk.

It was a beautiful September day in Lancaster, California—just a few weeks since the couple had enjoyed the sweet fellowship of Christian friends aboard a ministry cruise through Alaska's majestic inside passage. The trip had been unforgettable—a compelling reminder of God's magnificent power and goodness and a time to reflect on His blessings during their fifty-three years of marriage and ministry.

The weeks ahead would be filled with cross-country travel as Don preached in missions conferences to stir Christians and local churches to invest in missions around the world. But today, Don and Virginia enjoyed a quiet lunch together at home, not expecting that the next few moments would change their lives.

As she began to clear the kitchen table, Virginia suddenly felt lightheaded, and for several seconds, everything went black. Don, who was sitting just a few feet away, rushed to her side and escorted her to the couch, fearing this could be something serious.

Don's concerns for his wife had been growing. For several days he had noticed Virginia seemed to struggle with remembering things and with occasional disorientation. Her handwriting also had changed slightly. She just wasn't quite herself at times. And he would know, for this lovely lady had been his best friend, his companion, and his greatest delight in life for more than five decades.

They sat together on the couch for several moments as Don comforted his wife, contemplating what this physical issue might be and what should be done. He also prayed, and feared, and resolved, by God's grace, to help and care for his wife to the best of his ability, no matter what the future held. Together they resolved that the Lord is good—He had led them this far, and He would continue leading them. They would continue to trust Him.

A doctor's appointment that afternoon led to a CAT scan two days later, and on September 23 at 4:00 in the afternoon, the phone rang. It was the doctor with preliminary test results. The news was not good. The test revealed a large tumor growing on Virginia's brain. The mass could potentially be cancerous and would likely be inoperable. The prognosis was grim, but further testing was necessary before firm conclusions could be drawn.

Questions began to flood both of their hearts, and tears filled their eyes. Was this the beginning of the end? Would they soon be saying goodbye to one another until Heaven? How would the coming days unfold? Would they celebrate another anniversary? What was the Lord doing?

Abundant Grace

The news was devastating, but the grace of God was abundant. In those first moments together, Don and Virginia both immediately sensed the loving embrace of their Heavenly Father.

For several months the Lord had been reminding Don of Psalm 118:24, a verse from which Don had preached during the Alaska cruise: "*This is the day which the L*ord *hath made; we will rejoice and be glad in it.*" Over and over the verse came to mind with the fact that this was the hymn that the Lord Jesus sang the night before His betrayal and crucifixion. And once again, the Holy Spirit reminded him of this truth, seeming to say, "Don, I made this day, and I invite you to rejoice and be glad in Me." The Sisks wept, prayed, and rested in the Lord despite every human emotion crying out to the contrary.

The next morning came too quickly and, with it, another rush of overwhelming heaviness. Together, once again, Don and Virginia went to the Saviour they had faithfully walked with for so many years. Through tears they expressed their trust, claimed His grace, and chose to rejoice in this day the Lord had given them.

Moments later, a wonderful and unexpected outpouring of love and care began to unfold. In over fifty-three years of ministry, these two amazing servants of Christ had touched tens of thousands of lives across the globe. News of Virginia's illness began to spread, and it was as if the Holy Spirit instantly retraced five decades of ministry. In the thousands of places where the Sisks have ministered, memories of their influence were revived and grateful hearts began to share the burden. Suddenly, there were now thousands of Christian friends and co-laborers rising up in prayer, expressing love, and providing spiritual support.

Phone calls and e-mails began to come from around the world as people reached out to encourage these two giants of the faith. The Sisks were embraced by the grace of God personified through these to whom they had ministered. That evening, God gave Virginia a verse as she was reading her Bible that spoke to her circumstances. It was from the same Psalm Don had been meditating on: Psalm 118:17, "*I shall not die, but live, and declare the works of the Lord.*" What hope and strength this verse gave, and Virginia instantly claimed it for her trial.

A few moments later, Pastor Paul Chappell and a few of the pastoral staff and deacons of Lancaster Baptist Church visited the couple in their home. Don greeted them, but it was unusual to see this man without his larger-than-life happiness and gracious smile. His countenance was strong, but his heart was obviously heavy.

Mrs. Sisk greeted them with eyes moist with tears. In a voice barely louder than a whisper she said, "Pastor, I really don't want to die yet. I want to live longer so I can serve my Lord."

Everyone sat in the living room as Don shared the diagnosis. There was so much they didn't know, and the doctors weren't offering much hope. As he talked, his love for his wife was obvious in the way he held her close and gently comforted her. The image of their steadfast love in that moment was unforgettable.

The men gathered around Mrs. Sisk, anointed her with oil, and prayed earnestly that God grant her request to extend her life to serve Him and be glorified through her healing. In these same moments, Christian friends all over the world were praying as well. This would take a miracle.

A Choice to Rejoice

That weekend a fresh breath of encouragement arrived in the form of the Sisks' daughter, Renee, from Dayton, Ohio. Her presence lifted hearts and gave strength. Quite selflessly, Virginia had urged Don to keep his preaching commitments as much as possible, so the three travelled from Los Angeles to San Diego for a Sunday morning service at Canyon Ridge

Baptist Church. (That young church committed $75,000 to missions that morning after Don preached.)

After lunch, they drove back to Lancaster in time for the evening service, where they were greeted and encouraged by the church family. That evening, a church member named Shelly, who was also a dosimetrist (a member of a radiation oncology team) at Cedars-Sinai Medical Center in Beverly Hills, gave Don a note. In it was a business card and an offer to help arrange appointments with any specialist they might need to see. It was just one more detail that revealed the hand of God's answering prayer and moving on behalf of the Sisks.

The next day, God gave Virginia strength to endure an MRI without being sedated, and the family waited again for the test results. Late afternoon, the doctor confirmed with Don and Renee that the CAT scan had been correct, and the outlook was not good. They wept and prayed, asking God to give them strength in sharing the news with Virginia.

A short time later, the three sat quietly and made a very difficult choice. Early in this trial, the Sisks had made a simple decision in faith based upon Psalm 118:24: they would sing "This is the Day the Lord Hath Made" every single day, no matter what news they received or what hardship they faced. Against human logic, they determined to rejoice. And so in the face of circumstances that couldn't look any worse—hoping against hope and forcing back tears—they sang.

This is the day that the Lord hath made; I will rejoice and be glad in it. At this point, doctors offered no hope, but the Sisks refused to give up. Deciding to pursue any open door the Lord provided, Don pulled out Shelly's business card and made the phone call to Cedars-Sinai Medical Center's world renowned neurology department. Shelly called Don the next morning with great news: "I just met with Dr. Gabriel Hunt, one of the best neurologists in the country. He not only agreed to see Virginia, but he gave me his cell number and the number to his assistant and asked that you call to schedule the appointment for this Thursday morning."

It was evident that God's hand was moving in these circumstances, and prayers were already being answered.

Two days later, the Sisks met with Dr. Hunt for a four-hour appointment. He was a delightful man with a positive and hopeful spirit, and his obvious knowledge of their circumstances brought instant encouragement. He shared that after studying Virginia's MRI, it was his opinion that the tumor was not only benign, but that it could possibly be removed without any damage to her brain. He explained in detail the surgery he was recommending and the risks involved, and for the first time in days, the Sisks experienced a glimmer of hope. The outlook was still dire, and the chances of survival small, but the Lord gave a special peace that the surgery was the right step and Dr. Hunt was the right surgeon. It was scheduled for the following Friday—just eight days later.

In spite of the natural anxiety building about the upcoming surgery, that weekend was restful. The Sisks had a deep sense that God was leading in every step. Renee's husband, Tom, and their daughter, Rebecca, arrived to spend the weekend, and their presence brought sweet comfort and joy.

Virginia again urged Don to keep his preaching engagement for Sunday, so Don flew to Oakland to preach for the Heritage Baptist Church. Several souls came to Christ, and God gave a wonderful day.

Don arrived home late that night exhausted and contemplating the next few days. Would they be his last with Virginia at his side? In those quiet moments alone, he wrestled with emotions he had never faced before, and he made every conscious effort to continue rejoicing in the Lord and trusting His hand.

Labor Day brought a trip to the airport to see Tom and Rebecca off, then a quiet dinner with friends and a restful evening at home. Friends and family continued to call and write, expressing love and support, and on Wednesday, the Sisk's son, Tim, arrived. That night Don, Virginia, and their two children enjoyed a delightful dinner, as they had done so many times over the years. Don couldn't help but reflect on the years when their family was much younger and these dinners much more frequent. He marveled at his adult children, now serving the Lord and raising their own families.

On Thursday, one day before surgery, the Sisks checked into a hotel near the medical center. To their great delight, they were greeted by dear, longtime friends Pastor Lou Baldwin and his wife, Jeanette, who had flown to Los Angeles just to be with the Sisks during the surgery. This unexpected blessing brought great comfort.

After a time of prayer with them, Don and Virginia checked in at the medical center for another MRI and other tests in preparation for surgery. Through every procedure, Virginia displayed great strength and peace, and it was obvious the prayers of thousands were being answered again as God gave her heart an uncommon calm and quiet resolve.

Later that night, after a time of prayer, Don kissed his wife, put his head on the pillow, and wrestled with thoughts that this might be the last time he ever told her good night. While he chose to rest in faith, he could not deny fear, doubt, uncertainty, and sorrow were still present. While he was determined to be strong for his wife, he just wasn't sure if he was ready for Friday morning. He drifted off to sleep hoping and praying for a successful surgery.

This Is the Day

Early the next morning the Sisks awoke and, as was now their custom, sang "This is the Day that the Lord Hath Made." By 6:00 they were sitting in a hospital waiting room where they were greeted by Pastor Chappell and other friends. Together, they all prayed for God's guiding hand over the surgeon and His healing work in Virginia's body.

Fifteen minutes later, Virginia was led away to be prepared for her 7:15 AM surgery.

At 7:00 AM, Don, Tim, and Renee went with Pastor Chappell to pray with Virginia one more time. Don saw incredible bravery in his wife. It was obvious that God had given her a great peace in the midst of this storm. Together they prayed for strength and begged God to give healing. Don gently kissed his wife and returned to the waiting area to join the others in patient prayer.

Waiting and Remembering

Two hours later, a receptionist informed Don that the surgery (which was expected to last two hours)…had been delayed, and Virginia was just then being taken into surgery. Don noted that it was 9:00 AM and braced himself for the next two hours.

The following hours were the most difficult and traumatic of Don's entire life. Fifty-three years of marriage and ministry had all come down to one hundred twenty minutes. His and Virginia's life together had taken them to hundreds of churches in the States and to mission fields around the world. Their love and friendship was deep and abundant. Their commitment to Christ and His call upon their lives was unfailing. By God's grace, they had shared a life with very few regrets. But would this be the end?

Sitting quietly in the hospital waiting area, Don was cordial on the outside but enduring wave after wave of inexpressible emotion on the inside. He had chosen to rejoice in the Lord, yet he wrestled with knowing he might not see his precious wife again on earth. The wait was agonizing. The minutes passed slowly.

In those moments, Don couldn't help but remember all that the Lord had done in the past seven and a half decades of his life…

Two

THE LORD PROTECTED

1933–1945

Barely more than a country crossroad nestled among the rolling farm hills of western Kentucky, the city of Nortonville was home to only a few hundred people in the early 1900s. The town had begun as an Indian village and was later named after the wealthy W. E. Norton who settled there in the late 1800s. At the turn of the century, Nortonville boasted a general store, a tobacco warehouse, a train depot, a church, and a smattering of homes.

Things changed dramatically in 1902 when businessmen established a shaft coal mine in town and founded The Norton Coal Company. The next two decades brought growth, including a hotel, several dozen businesses, and eventually a town water system. Then, just as Nortonville reached its peak, the Great Depression left many residents out of work and struggling to get by.

In 1933, Earl and Beulah Sisk were residents of Nortonville and were just two of many Sisks in Western Kentucky at the time. Earl had been a coal miner at the Norton Coal Company since age fourteen. His life was hard, much of it spent underground, breathing coal dust and mining out a meager living—about twelve dollars per week for sixty hours of work—for his young family. Monday through Friday, Earl was buried in the blackness of the mine, and Saturday and Sunday, he was buried in the blackness of alcoholism and gambling.

Earl had lost his mother as a boy and had been reared by an abusive stepmother. When sober, he was a hard worker and a pleasant man, but alcohol made him angry and miserable, which meant the Sisk home was a difficult place much of the time.

Earl and Beulah had been married since 1916 and had already endured a difficult life together. They had raised their oldest daughter, lost their second as an infant, and were doing their best with their youngest children—two daughters and one son. Day to day, it was all they could do to pay the bills, feed the family, and make preparations for another baby on the way.

The soon-to-be family of seven lived in a simple house on Main Street, just blocks from the town's elementary school. The home had three small bedrooms, a kitchen, and a sitting room—no electricity and no indoor plumbing.

Into these meager and difficult circumstances God chose to bring Don Sisk into the world on May 30, 1933.

Not long after Don's first birthday, another sister was born, and eighteen months later, twins. One of Don's earliest memories is of the twins being very sick at birth and dying within their first two weeks of life. The death of infants was common in those days, and health care options in Nortonville were limited to home visits from the lone county physician, Dr. Johnson. The loss of children in infancy was a sorrow many families bore.

TWO—THE LORD PROTECTED

Beulah Sisk was an energetic, hardworking lady who took great care of her family. She was frugal, and she made family meals the main event in the Sisk home. From a large sack of flour and the grease from fried, lean back (a cheap pork meat), she would prepare homemade biscuits and gravy with eggs and pork nearly every morning. Meal times at the Sisk home provided some of the best and most vivid memories for all of the children.

More than seventy years later, Don distinctly recalls his mother's great cooking and her hard work in the kitchen: "We had some kind of potatoes nearly every meal (home fries, baked, mashed, potato cakes, etc.). We usually had either pinto or white beans or green beans. We always had a garden, and Mother canned many vegetables for winter."

As a small boy, Don especially loved his mom's chocolate cake—and in fact, had a near-death experience trying to get to one. It all began when he was alone in the kitchen and smelled a freshly baked cake. Beulah had placed it high atop the upper dish cabinet, presumably out of the reach of children, but she hadn't accounted for Don's boyish ingenuity. After all, boys are made for climbing, and a warm piece of chocolate cake is worth scaling whatever obstacles stand in the way. Don quietly and carefully mounted the countertop, using the upper dish cabinet as leverage.

In an instant, the cabinet came loose and crashed to the floor, sending dishes, cabinetry, and—unfortunately—cake to the floor in a clanging, glass-shattering disaster. Unharmed but terrified at what he had done, Don ran to another room and hid. The rest of the family, startled by the noise, rushed into the kitchen and panicked, fearing that Don was buried under the pile of glass, wood, and cake.

Don played the scene as only a mischievous boy could. Rather than run to show his family he was unhurt he quietly waited, and by the time his family found him a few moments later, they were so relieved that he wasn't dead that they didn't even discipline him for destroying the kitchen or the cake. Though cake-less, he was quite satisfied, for his near-death experience had caused enough ruckus and panic that he avoided getting in trouble in the process. He still sports an impish grin when recalling this story.

A Life-Altering Tragedy

When Don was about six years old, his dad was involved in a tragic mining accident. The coal mines were dangerous, and accidents and deaths were common. The shaft Earl was working in collapsed around him, trapping him under hundreds of pounds of rock and dirt and wounding him badly. Fellow miners were eventually able to dig him out, but his injuries were critical. Emergency services were non-existent in that day, so Earl was loaded into the back of a pickup truck and rushed over twenty miles of dirt and gravel roads to the closest hospital in Hopkinsville.

Doctors discovered that Earl's legs and hips were broken and he had serious internal injuries. He was not expected to survive, but Earl clung to life. Days turned into weeks and months, and still he held on. The Sisks didn't own a car, so nearly every day Beulah hired someone to drive her to the hospital to visit her husband.

Doctors did everything they could, with little improvement. In fact, during his two-month hospital stay, Earl shed seventy pounds from his solid two hundred-pound frame. He was finally released to his home, where doctors expected him to eventually pass away from his injuries. The frail, skeletal man that came home from the hospital barely resembled Don's once-strong father, but Earl fought to survive and recover. Little by little, he began to heal—perhaps due to the tender love and home cooking of his good wife.

The Sisk family struggled financially following Earl's accident. The older children were able to find occasional work, and Don's older brother found a job opportunity through President Roosevelt's "New Deal" building roads and dams. This, combined with a bit of credit from the coal company and the help of friends and family, allowed the Sisks to make ends meet during these lean days. Then one day, as Don was in the company grocery store alone, the store owner pulled him aside and told him the Sisks had reached their limit and could no longer purchase their weekly necessities on credit. He didn't have the heart to speak to Beulah or the older siblings, so he asked Don to tell his family. It was a horrible duty to place on a boy. Don never forgot how it felt to break that difficult news to his mother. This made the months to follow even more uncertain for the entire family.

After several weeks at home, Earl's condition began to improve. At first, he took just a few steps each day, but within six months he was almost completely recovered and even began working again at the coal mine. But after nine months out of work, it was a long time before Earl brought home any cash for the family. Most of his earnings were withheld to pay the debts that had accrued during his injury.

Early Education

Don had a rough start to his school days. The school was less than four blocks from his home on Main Street, and each morning Beulah would walk him to school and drop him off. The only problem was, he didn't want to go.

In true Tom Sawyer style, as soon as his mother turned to leave, Don would dart across the schoolyard to the back alley, which ran parallel to Main Street behind the row of homes. He would run all the way back home, beating his mother there every time. His victory wouldn't last long, as she would then beat him—all the way back to school. But little boys have short memories, and so the next morning the whole ordeal was repeated—and continued every day of the first week of first grade. Don finally settled into school, but it was a while before he actually enjoyed it. Several years later, Don's nephew, the son of Earl Jr., came home from school and complained to his father, "I don't know why I am going to school. All they do is read and write there, and I can't do either!" When Don heard that, he wished he had thought like that when he was in the first grade.

After first grade, Don's next three years in school were more pleasant. Each day the teacher read the Bible to the class and led in a time of prayer, giving Don his first exposure to God's Word. On Sundays, Don and the other children his age would occasionally walk to Sunday school, where seeds of faith and Bible truth were planted. The tender compassion of the Sunday school teachers stood in stark contrast to the lifestyle of his father. Earl had made a half-hearted confession of faith a few years before when a local preacher visited the family during Earl's illness. Perhaps because of his condition and his desperation for healing, Earl's heart was briefly softened toward the things of God, but as soon as he was able to walk again, he returned to the old habits of drinking, gambling, and neglecting his family.

Move to Mannington

After Don's tenth birthday, Earl took a new job at the Sterling Coal Company, which moved the family six miles from Nortonville to Mannington, Kentucky—at the time a rather infamous town. Mannington was situated in one of the few "wet" counties (ironically named Christian County) in the region, and it was known for its bootleggers, illegal whisky, taverns, and liquor stores. In those days, one might have called Mannington the "drinking capital of western Kentucky."

The Sisk house in Mannington was small—just four rooms. In fact, throughout Don's childhood, he never lived in a home with more than five rooms total. The Mannington school was even smaller, with just one room for the first through third grades and one room for the fourth through eighth grades. And while school days in Mannington provided mostly pleasant memories, the older teenage boys were bullies and troublemakers. In fact, between Don's fourth and six grade years, four different teachers quit out of sheer exasperation with unruly students.

But when Ruby May Poe became the schoolteacher, even some of the most roguish boys discovered a brand new inspiration for good behavior. On the first day of school, Ruby May's father walked in with a long paddle in his hands—complete with five freshly drilled holes at the tip. He had fashioned it for Ruby May to use on any boys who became unruly, but he threatened to paddle the boys with it himself if they challenged her authority. No one doubted his fierce sincerity, and suddenly, good behavior in the Mannington school was the order of the day. Ruby May's firm discipline at first troubled some of the parents, but over time she won their hearts because the students improved in behavior and academics. For Don, the discipline was just a fact of life. Every child looks for ways to play authorities against each other, but in his case, this was a losing battle. His parents always sided with the teacher, and a whipping at school always meant another whipping at home.

Ruby May was Don's teacher from fifth to eighth grade and was a special lady in young Don's life. She was a great teacher, and she took a special interest in Don. She helped him in school, encouraged him in life, and invested time and care into his life.

World War II from Kentucky

Don was still in upper elementary school in December of 1941 when a tragedy struck on the national front. As he was listening to the radio at his sister's home, just a few blocks from his own, news of the bombing of Pearl Harbor came over the air. Not long after, America declared war, and life took a dramatic turn for most of the country. Don's older brother, Earl Thomas Jr., was one of the first men drafted into the army from their community. Don was almost nine years old when he said goodbye to his older brother in January of 1942. Earl Jr. spent six weeks in basic training, was shipped off to Europe, and returned three years later at the end of the war.

A world at war and a nation under attack leaves deeply impressed memories within a preteen boy. While Earl Jr. was overseas, it was Don's job to run to the Mannington post office every day in hopes that a letter would arrive from Europe. Communication was painfully slow, and on a weekly basis, other neighbors received news of the death of a son or father in combat. Months would pass between letters from Earl Jr., and Earl Sr. and Beulah would often weep when Don returned from the post office empty handed. The wait was excruciating.

During the war, the nation was united in the cause of defeating the Japanese and the Nazis. Families willingly embraced government-imposed rationing of food and commodities, realizing a much greater sacrifice was being made on the front lines of battle. Necessities like meat, gasoline, and clothing could only be obtained through government-issued ration stamps. These stamps became a sort of currency that allowed the government to control supply and demand during wartime. Americans were allowed to purchase just one pair of shoes per year, and government posters encouraged people to preserve their resources. Determined to do what little he could to help fight the war and help his brother stay alive overseas, Don would go out to search for scraps of iron or tin that he could turn in at a recycling center for a few pennies. He knew those scraps of metal would be used to make tanks, bullets, ships, and supplies, and he was glad he could do something.

Don also helped cultivate his family's victory garden and watched his mother put up the harvest in canning jars for winter months. Nearly every home during those years had a victory garden to help conserve food and provide families with fresh vegetables. In fact, across the country, Americans planted twenty million victory gardens that produced 40 percent of America's vegetable supply during those years.

America was united, the world divided, and ten-year-old Don Sisk was discovering a desire to be immersed in a cause greater than himself—a character trait that would never leave his heart. His father was often neglectful, his mother hard-working and gracious, his older brother fighting a war overseas, and Miss Ruby May Poe investing her heart and life into his—what did it all mean? At the time, there was no way of seeing the bigger picture, but in retrospect, God was at work protecting and gently forming a young man for an eternal cause.

Don's twelfth birthday was a few weeks after the surrender of the Germans, and a few months later America dropped the atomic bomb, which swiftly led to the Japanese surrender. The war was finally over, and Americans celebrated. And the Sisks celebrated in a special way at being reunited with Earl Jr.—and his new fiancé. While overseas, Earl Jr. had begun writing to the sister of a fellow soldier, and a few weeks after returning home from war, he went to West Virginia and married his sweetheart.

Divine Providence

Often the protection of God and the infinite nature of His plan are more clearly seen in retrospect. To relate the next event that showed God's hand in Don's life, it is helpful to go back a few years to 1941. In that year Earl Sr. was mining coal, Beulah was raising their family, and Don was attending elementary school with Miss Ruby May as his teacher; but across the Atlantic Ocean, a man named Alexander Fleming and a team of scientists were making what would become perhaps the most significant medical discovery of the twentieth century. Their research reached America that year, but it wasn't until 1944 that scientists were finally able to effectively mass-produce this miracle—just in time for our story to continue.

In 1945, as America was beginning to heal from the war, twelve-year-old Don was stricken with a life-threatening case of pneumonia. He spent many days in bed, suffering and often unconscious, barely clinging to life. Alexander Fleming's miracle drug—penicillin—had only just reached the hands of country doctors in western Kentucky. The experimental release of the drug divinely converged with Don's sickness. Had God not allowed Dr. Johnson of Mannington to administer penicillin to this boy, his story might well have ended right here. But God had big plans for Don Sisk. He was molding a servant and preparing a soldier.

Isn't God's hand amazing? His ways are truly beyond comprehension. As Don approached his thirteenth birthday, God had already been mightily at work in His life, and the boy didn't even know it. Earl Sr. was unwittingly used of God to thicken the skin and strengthen the resolve of a man that would one day endure great testing. Beulah was used of God to cultivate a gracious, servant's spirit and a hardworking character that would one day labor with uncommon grace and sacrifice. Ruby May was used to touch a boyish heart that would one day beat with Christ-like tenderness and gentle compassion for the souls of men all over the world. Earl Jr. was valiantly fighting so that the free world might continue; and that his younger brother might one day reach it with the gospel of eternal freedom. And Alexander Fleming was used to provide a cure that would spare a life in the back hills of Kentucky that this life might reach countless others.

Three
THE LORD SAVED

1945–1950

At age twelve, a few months after God intervened and healed Don, he attended a revival meeting in a Methodist Church in Mannington, Kentucky. An old-fashioned Methodist preacher, by the name of Everett Grace, stood and faithfully sounded out the Word of God for several nights. On one particular night, he passionately described in detail the crucifixion of Jesus Christ. It was the first time that Don had heard such a clear and vivid account of what Christ endured. Although this message was convicting, Don's young heart did not understand why Jesus had to face such a tragic death. He understood the facts, but the reasons for Christ's death never penetrated his thinking. He left the church service that night with conviction in his heart but still did not understand his need for a personal Saviour.

God continued to place Don in situations where the gospel was presented, and the Holy Spirit continued to use the seeds planted to soften his heart and draw him ever closer to understanding the gospel message. At the age of thirteen, he was at home one day when someone knocked on the door. When he answered, a woman named Miss Helen greeted him. Miss Helen was a courageous servant of the Lord who humbly traveled door to door in the town of Mannington to invite children to vacation Bible school. Amazingly, this woman, in her early twenties, ran this vacation Bible school by herself.

Mannington didn't offer much excitement to a thirteen-year-old boy, so Don decided to be a part of Miss Helen's vacation Bible school. It was well attended by the other kids in town, and Miss Helen enthusiastically told them all of Christ's love for them. Don was taught to read the Bible and appreciate the many exciting stories within it.

Each day, Miss Helen concluded the VBS by singing, "Come into my heart, Lord Jesus." As she did, Don could sense the Holy Spirit tugging at his heart for salvation. He wanted to be saved, but he wasn't sure he was ready to live for Jesus Christ.

Don's longing to be saved was greatly increased because of Miss Helen's influence. He had seen plenty of the emptiness of sin and the despair of life without Christ, but one thing that continued to hold him back was the poor testimony of professing Christians. He saw many "believers" who appeared to be living in drudgery and oppression. Their lack of joy made the Christian life unattractive and unappealing to Don. He reasoned, "If that is what being a Christian does to someone, I'll wait until I'm much older and near death to accept Christ. That way I can enjoy my life!" But Miss Helen was different. She was full of the joy of the Lord, and her gracious spirit was compelling. With her, Jesus was more than a distant deity; He was a present reality. Jesus was obviously *everything* to her. She demonstrated not merely a lip service to Him, but a genuine love for Him. And her testimony caused Don to desire this same genuine joy and authentic relationship with Christ.

The High School Years

With the truth of the gospel still lingering in his heart, Don graduated from eighth grade and began attending Nortonville High School in 1947. The public high schools of this era were quite different from those of today, especially in western Kentucky. In many ways, Nortonville High School resembled the Christian schools of today. Morality and faith were held in high regard, and the students were encouraged to pray, read their Bibles, and uphold a high standard of dress and lifestyle.

In high school, God continued to strategically place influencers in Don's life. One such providential relationship was Mrs. Gladish, who taught algebra and geometry—two of Don's favorite classes. Mrs. Gladish was a godly Christian woman who loved her students. She didn't speak much about her faith, but she exhibited a daily walk with the Lord. Don recalls her sweet way of encouraging others and expressing the love of Christ. He knew she was a Christian, and her life taught Don that a person's walk speaks louder than her talk.

Mr. Skaggs, the principal of Nortonville High School, was also influential in Don's life. Although unsaved, he was a dedicated teacher who showed great care and concern for his students. In spite of the fact that Mr. Skaggs owned a vehicle and could have driven himself to school each morning, he chose to brave the confines of a bus filled with rowdy teenagers each day. He used this time to encourage and mentor the students personally. His selflessness and desire to be a help was a great inspiration to Don. This man's influence impressed upon Don's heart that life was really all about loving and serving others.

Love at First Sight?

There are relatively few moments in life that are life-changing, but the day that Don Sisk laid eyes on Virginia Carlton was one of those days.

It was the middle of his sophomore year. Don was sixteen years old and on the basketball team. On this day, practice had begun and Don was on the court running drills with his team. Don tried to focus as the coach was calling plays, but his attention was divided. Someone had caught his eye. He noticed a petite brunette to the side of the court—someone he hadn't seen before, and suddenly he was having trouble focusing on basketball. Unaware of the impact of her presence and the struggle she had created for Don, Virginia stood innocently watching practice. Moments later, their eyes met for the first time. It was a moment that Don will never forget. His heart skipped a beat, and suddenly his mind was racing with a new range of unfamiliar feelings. There was something very special about this girl. He didn't even know her name, but somehow he knew instantly she would someday be his wife.

Love at first sight? Perhaps. Boyish infatuation? Probably. Divine providence? Absolutely.

After noticing her, Don realized that his cousin, Connie, was standing near her. When he later asked Connie if she knew the girl, Connie replied that Virginia was one of her best friends. A few days passed before Don had an opportunity to speak to Virginia personally. He saw her as he walked into a café near the school, and she was sitting alone with an empty chair next to her. When he greeted her and asked if he could sit with her, she was surprised that he knew her name. As he told her his, she answered, "Oh, I know *you*...." Don was flattered, and his heart swelled with the courage to continue the relationship.

That day was the beginning of a beautiful friendship and a lifetime love. Don and Virginia purposefully made every effort to spend more time together, from sitting with each other at school to being together at school activities. They shared a study hall two days a week and interacted through the Baptist Training Union Group of Nortonville Baptist Church. Their teen courtship blossomed, and Don started walking Virginia home.

At this time, there still weren't many automobiles in Mannington, and for that they were both thankful. They cherished the mile-long walk together each day, and grew to know each other very well.

Don was impressed by Virginia. Not only was she a good student, but she was a great athlete as well. He enjoyed watching her play basketball, and described her as a "scrappy guard." She was beautiful, quiet but responsive, with a gentle spirit, a personal confidence, and a great personality that would be a great asset to their future life and ministry together.

As their relationship progressed, Don eventually began visiting Virginia at home with her family. He was a bit fearful of her mother and father but always impressed with both of them. And he was motivated by the knowledge that he wanted Virginia as his wife. She was everything he could have dreamed of. He was hooked, and he loved it.

You Should Be a Preacher

Ironically, the Lord implanted the idea of being a preacher into Don's heart before he was even saved, and he used a high school speech teacher by the name of Mrs. Puttman to do it. During an eleventh grade speech class, the students were given the assignment of preparing a speech that they would be required to give to the class.

Don chose to give his speech on Samson and Delilah. His decision wasn't based on the leading of the Holy Spirit; it was much simpler than that. It just so happened that the assignment coincided with the recent release of the major motion picture "Samson and Delilah," a 1949 hit from the well-known movie director, Cecil B. DeMille. Don had just been to the Hopkinsville theatre to see the movie and figured the story would make for an easy speech because the details were fresh in his memory.

As Don delivered his speech, Mrs. Puttman was apparently impressed. When he finished she said, "Don, you should be a preacher." That statement stuck with him for many years.

A Basketball Fan at Heart

Don's love for sports was cultivated in high school under the mentorship of Pete Wagner, the basketball coach at Nortonville High School. Don was ecstatic when he tried out for the team his freshman year and made it. He played more on the junior varsity team than the varsity, but loved the sport nonetheless. Throughout high school he always dressed out for the varsity games despite the little playing time he enjoyed. He was just happy to support the team and share in the friendships and memories of high school athletics. During his senior year, the Nortonville basketball team finished the season with twenty-eight wins and only two losses. They nearly went to the state finals but lost in the district tournament. This time on the basketball team was formational to his character in many ways, and through it God gave him some wonderful lifetime friendships.

During Don's freshman year, Coach Wagner took the whole team to see the number-one rated University of Kentucky play number-two rated Bradley University at home in their new field house in Owensboro, Kentucky. Owensboro was about fifty miles away, and this was one of the first times Don ever travelled beyond the borders of his hometown. The game was intense and the whole adventure initiated Don into a dyed-in-the-wool, lifetime University of Kentucky fan.

A New Beginning

Of the many influences and great experiences of high school, nothing compares to the day Don's friend invited him to attend a Youth for Christ meeting. Youth for Christ meetings began after World War II through the work of evangelical leaders who desired to reach youth with the gospel message. In the late 1940s these meetings grew and eventually spread throughout America. On a Monday morning in 1949, in the middle of Don's junior year, his friend, Bill Welch, invited him to attend a meeting with him that Saturday night.

Other than Virginia, Bill was Don's best friend, so the decision to say "yes" was an easy one. But later in the week Don began to have some doubts about attending. Bill was a Christian, and it was obvious by the name of the meeting that there would be other Christians present. Don knew that he was not a Christian, and he was certain he would stick out like a sore thumb. The thought of attending intimidated him, so he began to look for a viable excuse to back out. He thought through every possible scenario and explanation, but he simply couldn't bring himself to let down his best friend.

Don had been to Christian meetings, revival meetings, and camp meetings. He had heard the gospel on several occasions. He knew he wasn't saved, but he still wasn't exactly sure how to be saved. He thought about his eternal destiny often, and he remembered the love of godly people in his life. He knew he was a sinner, and would often lie awake at night and think, "I hope I don't die tonight. If I do, I will probably wind up in Hell." These thoughts were not what Don liked to dwell on, so he continually pushed them away. But God kept nudging them forward again.

By Saturday morning, the day of the Youth for Christ meeting, insecurities and fears about the night still swirled in Don's mind. Throughout the day, God continued speaking to his heart, using Don's own thoughts to help him realize his need for a Saviour long before the meeting began. Don began to consider his hopelessness, lack of direction, poverty, and more predominantly, the fact that if he died at that moment he would spend eternity in Hell. He recalled the times he had wanted to become a Christian. He considered the joy of the genuine Christians he had encountered throughout his life. The wrestling match with the Holy Spirit intensified all day, until Don finally decided he was done searching for an excuse not to go to the meeting.

Furthermore, Don determined he was going to church and was going to be saved that night. Though he didn't fully comprehend all that "being saved" meant, he knew that when the preacher gave the invitation later that night, he would be the first one to step out.

Essentially, through the simple invitation of a friend, the Holy Spirit compiled years of collective "seed sowing" in Don's heart. Years of convicting exposure to the gospel and Christ-like Christians came to fruition in the privacy of a Saturday afternoon wrestling match with God. The quiet but convicted heart of a teenage young man finally determined to surrender to God's call of repentance and salvation. Little did all the "seed-sowers" of Don's past realize what a fantastic harvest their efforts would yield. Little did Bill Welch know what his simple invitation to his friend would mean over the next seventy years.

Don sat through the sermon that evening eagerly awaiting the end of the message so he could step forward. When the preacher finished and the invitation song began, Don determinedly stepped into the aisle and headed to the front. A local pastor named Gifford Berry followed him down the aisle and asked, "Don, what are you coming for?" He simply replied, "I need to be saved."

Pastor Berry took Don aside, opened the Bible, and showed Don that he was a sinner deserving of eternal separation from God. He explained that Jesus had died for his sins, and then he told Don, "If you would pray and ask the Lord to save you, He will." That night Don bowed his head and prayed a simple prayer: "Dear Lord, I know I'm a sinner. I can't save myself. I have tried that. I'm trusting You as my Saviour."

There was no fanfare, no applause. But in that instant, peace came into Don's heart unlike anything he had ever known or experienced. He was glad and thankful he had finally surrendered to God's conviction and accepted Jesus as his personal Saviour.

Later that night, he lay his head down on the same pillow where so many other nights he had wrestled with doubt and fear. That same place where he had so often considered his eternal fate was now a place of complete peace. Where fear had reigned and doubts had tossed, he now experienced the wonderful awareness of Christ in his life. He cherished the thought, "If I die tonight, I'll wake up in Heaven."

Don's decision to trust Christ was the defining moment of his entire life. He has never gotten over the peace and joy that entered into his life that night. He has never tired of telling others the gospel message. He has never lost the delight of helping others pray that simple sinner's prayer.

And from that moment, his life was forever and completely transformed for the glory of God.

A Growing Passion for the Gospel

When he awoke the Sunday morning after his salvation, Don's first thought was, "I'm going to church." He attended a small Methodist church in Mannington—the only church in town.

The Sunday school class that morning was more interesting than any other he could remember. To him, everything about church had changed. But in reality it was Don Sisk who had changed. Things that at one time meant very little now meant a great deal— from the songs and the spirit of the people singing to the reading of the Scripture. Suddenly, Don had a new and growing appetite for the Word of God and spiritual songs. Every "first Christian experience" held real meaning and significance as his newly saved heart began to feast on God's grace and truth.

At first Don really struggled with the idea of witnessing to others. Like most, he was timid. When he arrived at school on Monday at least half a dozen of his friends told him how grateful they were he had gotten saved and that they had been praying for his salvation for quite a while. But it took him several days just to tell his parents or anyone else that he had trusted Christ.

Shortly after his conversion, the Nortonville Baptist Church held a revival meeting. Most of Don's good friends attended this church, including Bill Welch and Virginia Carlton. A man from Texas named Reverend Wright preached that week, and his messages spoke deeply to Don's heart.

Pastor Jack Ratliff was the pastor of this humble church. He was a student at Louisville Seminary, and he and his wife, Winona, were preparing to be missionaries to Peru. It was during the Thursday night service that Don went forward and told Pastor Ratliff he would like to become a member of the Nortonville Baptist Church.

The pastor took Don's request seriously. He showed Don Ephesians 2:8–9, *"For by grace are ye saved through faith; and that not of yourselves: it is the gift of God: Not of works, lest any man should boast."* Pastor Ratliff asked Don to memorize these verses and quote them to him the next day. This was the pastor's way of making sure Don understood what it meant to be saved.

A few days later, Don was baptized and joined the church. This public profession of Christ touched the heart of Don's good friend, Donnie Holmes, who also expressed a desire to be saved. Pastor Ratliff and Reverend Wright went to visit Donnie later that week and led him to Jesus Christ.

This was the first soul that Don directly influenced toward the Lord, and the event sparked something in his heart. There was something incredible about being a part of someone else's coming to Christ. Through this, Don's desire to help others hear the gospel and be saved became a growing passion.

A Surrendered Life

Through the generosity of Pastor Ratliff, Don was able to go to camp the summer before his senior year of high school. He stayed in the same room with Pastor Ratliff and learned much about the Bible during the week.

Being away from home was an awesome adventure, but the best part of camp was being immersed in a godly environment. For a young man growing up in a non-Christian home, it was a taste of Heaven to be suddenly surrounded by godly influences, Bible teaching, and joyful Christians for an entire week. It was an experience Don never forgot, as he began to understand and embrace what it meant to be a Christian and to live the Christian life. He even began to envision having a Christian home and raising a Christian family.

During this week of camp, Don met Jerome O. Williams, a godly man in his early seventies who had spent more than forty years serving as a missionary to Africa. Don knew very little about other nations or continents, but he was intrigued by the stories told by this brave veteran missionary. Later that week, Don completely surrendered his life to the will of God. He didn't know what that would mean or where that would lead. He only knew that he longed to live a life of eternal value for the Lord Jesus.

After returning from camp, Don wrote Virginia (who had been saved as a young girl in Sunday school) a letter explaining what the Lord had done in his life. Although just a senior in high school, he already understood that the call of Jesus Christ should come before every other relationship and desire of his heart. With real depth and maturity, as a teen young man, he wrote:

> You know, I'm not sure that God wants me to be a missionary, but I'm also not sure that He doesn't. Virginia, if you would not be willing to be a missionary, it may not be a good idea for us to continue our relationship.

This was a big step and a risky one, for he certainly didn't want to lose his relationship with Virginia. But he also knew that he would follow God with his life, above all other desires and pursuits.

Not long after, Virginia wrote back:

Don, if God wants you to be a missionary, I would be glad to go anywhere God would have you go.

Needless to say, he breathed a long sigh of relief.

Four

THE LORD TAUGHT

1951–1953

It was the era of poodle skirts and flat tops, *I Love Lucy* and the introduction of color television, conservatism and anti-communism. And it was the age in which Don and Virginia Sisk began to build their future together.

Don's senior year of high school flew by and before he knew it, graduation was upon him. At eighteen, he stood at the crossroads of adulthood. He had been saved roughly a year and a half, and his walk with the Lord was growing daily. With God as his guide, he faced the future with real hope and anticipation. He yearned to serve the Lord with his life and was determined to remain fully surrendered.

Meanwhile, Don and Virginia had grown deeper in love with each passing day. Don attended Austin Peay State College after graduation, and as the first year of college came to a close, the young couple decided it was time to say "I do."

And so on Saturday afternoon, June 7, 1952, Don and Virginia made a lifetime covenant before God at the Nortonville Baptist Church, where they had attended together and grown in Christ. To both of them, being married in this church was representative of their desire to build their new family upon the unshakeable foundation of Jesus Christ.

Having a large wedding was unheard of in Nortonville, and because they had little money, Don and Virginia's wedding was far from extravagant; yet, it was a magnificent celebration of two Christians who loved the Lord with all their hearts. Only three other people attended apart from the bride and groom: Pastor Ratliff and the couple's two witnesses—Don's best friend, Donnie Holmes, and Virginia's best friend, Connie Love. Pastor Ratliff read a simple wedding ceremony, led the couple through their vows, and pronounced them husband and wife.

Although Don had very little, after the ceremony, he gave Pastor Ratliff the most he could—five dollars—for performing the service. Pastor Ratliff knew their financial situation and gave the money back. This gesture meant so much to Don, that since then, he has never once accepted money for performing a wedding ceremony.

This day marked the beginning of a truly wonderful life together. There were bumps along the way just like any marriage, but with their faith in God and commitment to each other, Don and Virginia persevered through every trial.

As Don reflects back on the beginning stages of their marriage, he would make one change. Specifically, he regrets not giving more preparation to marriage before the wedding. The idea of having premarital counseling never crossed his mind, but he realizes now that this could have greatly enhanced the first few years of their marriage.

Even so, there is one thing Don would *not* change. Specifically, the person he married. Don never doubted for one second that Virginia was the woman God chose specially for him. Two things were certain between them from the beginning, and these two things held them together through every hardship. The first was that the Lord had led them together. The second was that they chose to love each other. They saw love as a choice, not merely a fleeting emotion. These two core values have made their relationship virtually indestructible and have allowed for continued growth in love and grace.

Enjoying Life Together

Shortly after their wedding, Don and Virginia moved to Gary, Indiana. Don's parents and brother had recently moved there as well, so they were glad to be near family. They had very few belongings, which made the transition easy. As a newly married couple, they lived off a meager income, yet they were happy and content with the love the Lord had given them for each other. Don would later say, "Although we had nothing materially speaking, we had everything because we had each other."

Being an ambitious man, Don quickly got a job in construction for a couple of weeks until the Lord opened an opportunity at Keen's Foundry, which specialized in making small engine housings to aid during the Korean War. The hourly wage at the foundry was one dollar, which meant Don made roughly forty dollars a week.

Soon after settling into their new home, they began searching for a Bible-believing Baptist church to call home. Finding a solid place to grow in Christ was a priority, and they looked prayerfully for the right place. One Sunday morning they decided to visit Black Oak Baptist Church. From the first few moments of the service, the newlyweds knew that this little church would become their church family.

Black Oak Baptist was different than their church in Kentucky in several respects. For one, unlike Pastor Ratliff, Pastor W. E. Jones had received little formal training. After Pastor Jones was saved, he could barely read, but, hungry for God's Word, he quickly taught himself. He may not have had much time in the classroom, but it was apparent that Pastor Jones spent ample time with the Lord. The Lord's power enveloped this man of God as he preached, and as a result, blessings were unfolding at this ministry that Don and Virginia had never experienced before.

There was something distinct about Pastor Jones' preaching. He not only preached the encouraging truths from God's Word, but he also embraced the sterner truths. He preached on the love of God without glossing over the holiness of God. He preached about biblical separation, of which Don and Virginia knew very little. In their church in Kentucky, nearly all the men would stand outside and smoke cigarettes in the minutes between Sunday school and church. And while Pastor Ratliff had an enormous impact on Don's life, living a separated Christian life was something he rarely preached. At Black Oak, Don and Virginia began to learn that a biblical life impacts both the heart and the behavior. The longer they attended Black Oak Baptist, the more the truth about separation began to penetrate their hearts.

One specific incident was used by God to bring Don to commit to distinctive biblical living. He had never been taught that it was wrong to smoke. In fact, he had begun smoking at a young age, so quitting would not come easy. He had tried to stop on many different occasions, but he never seemed to have the personal discipline it required, and he would inevitably fall back into the habit. Every Wednesday night Black Oak held a prayer meeting, and often, instead of a sermon, members would take turns leading a testimony meeting. One Sunday night after Don and Virginia had been members for a while, Pastor Jones asked Don to lead the testimony meeting the following Wednesday. Don was more than willing to do so, but knowing he had cigarettes in his pocket presented a problem in his conscience.

The church had recently hosted a revival meeting, during which several people had been saved and God had worked miraculously in the hearts of the church family. As Don thought about leading the Wednesday service, God brought a particular testimony to his mind. He recalled a man who shared, "After I got saved the other night, I couldn't sleep. So I got up, lit a cigarette and began to smoke and I put that out and went back to bed and still couldn't sleep. So, I got up and began to think about what had happened to me, and I started to light another cigarette. All of a sudden it seemed like God spoke to me and said, 'You don't need that anymore.' Thank God, from that time until now, I have not smoked another cigarette."

The man's words had replayed over and over in Don's mind, and they came back to mind now as Pastor Jones had asked him to lead the next prayer meeting. As he and Virginia drove home that night, he made a decision about his cigarettes. He drew his pack out of his pocket and confidently threw them out the window as he told Virginia, "I will never smoke another cigarette again."

Ever the voice of reason, Virginia replied, "You've quit before, Don."

"Oh yes," Don answered, but with a fresh excitement from his decision and a new conviction in his heart, he continued, "but I have never quit like this. It's not a matter of *me* quitting this time. It's a matter of what God has told me to do."

The desire to smoke did not dissipate overnight as Don had hoped it would. He had heard testimonies of people who quit drinking and never wanted another taste or those who quit smoking and never craved another cigarette. It wasn't this way for Don. He struggled with the temptation for months. Every time someone lit a cigarette in his presence, he wanted badly to give in. But one day someone gave him good advice: "Put a New Testament in the pocket where you used to keep your cigarettes. That way, every time you reach for your cigarettes, you'll remember you have the Word of God and you don't need those anymore." Don took the advice, and, although it was not easy at first, this strategy helped. From the day his cigarettes flew out the window, Don never tasted another.

Don and Virginia continued learning about biblical separation, and when they came to understand the truth and importance of living distinctively as Christians, they committed to it for the testimony of Jesus Christ. The young couple allowed the Lord to speak to their hearts and mold them for His honor and glory.

True holiness and usefulness do not come without yielded hearts, and Don and Virginia reaped multiplied spiritual blessings because of their willingness to obey God's leading in their lives during these early years together.

How differently their story might have unfolded had they resisted God's conviction and lordship in these simple areas of lifestyle. Their tender, willing hearts were like good soil that God would cultivate for many years to come. That spirit of surrender has followed them for the remainder of their journey and impacted countless tens of thousands of people, all over the world, to love and follow Jesus Christ.

Growing in the Grace of Generosity

From the beginning of their life together, Don and Virginia were forced to live by faith. Don had very little income, and they had to find creative ways to get by. For instance, they didn't own an automobile, but instead relied upon others for rides to church and work.

One Sunday, Pastor Jones preached a simple message on tithing. He said that one-tenth of everything God gives belongs to Him. That morning, Don went forward, knelt down at the altar, and committed to give to the Lord through the local church at least one-tenth of everything he received from that day forward.

A few moments later, Pastor Jones announced Don's step of obedience to the church.

Sharing the story later, Don says with a boyish smile and a twinkle in his eye, "When I committed to tithe, the treasurer of the church did not jump up and down and say, 'Praise God, now that Don's going to tithe, our financial problems are over!' Frankly, my tithe was only four dollars per week, which probably meant very little to the church. But this decision meant a great deal to the Lord and to Virginia and me. It impacted our hearts in being willing to sacrifice each week out of our love for the Lord. And once we started giving as God commanded, we learned that He would provide for our needs just as He promised."

Not long after their decision to tithe, the Sisks were able to purchase their first automobile, and Don received an increase in salary. After having worked as a laborer for some time, he was encouraged by his supervisor to learn the job of a core maker in the factory. This job consisted of operating a machine where the cores for the molds in the foundry would be used. This new job was one of the few in the foundry that paid by commission. Don's payment each day was dependent on how many cores he produced. The position quickly became a channel of God's provision. It didn't take Don long to learn the job well and become productive. His incredible proficiency soon made him one of the highest paid employees in the entire foundry. Where the average yearly salary in 1952 and 1953 was $3,700, Don was making $8,500. To this day, Don attributes this blessing to his faith decision to begin tithing off of a much smaller income. He discovered then, and many times since, that we cannot out-give God.

By the summer of 1953 and their first wedding anniversary, Don and Virginia had relocated to Gary, Indiana, begun a thriving new career, surrendered themselves in greater consecration to God, learned to begin tithing, purchased their first automobile, and were trusting God at a whole new level.

These small seeds of growth and faith would reap an amazing harvest in the decades to come, all by God's wonderful grace.

Five

THE LORD ANSWERED

1953

In 1939, Harvard Medical School began a seventy-five-year long study following the life paths of 268 physically and mentally healthy young men. The Grant Study, as it came to be known, was exhaustive and covered the outcomes of every aspect of every season of the men's lives. The goal of the study was to identify the "sources of happiness," or to determine how and why some men enjoyed their lives and aged well while others did not. In the 2012 book, *Triumphs of Experience*, George Valliant, who directed the study for more than thirty years, summarized the seventy-five-year findings in a few profound words: "Happiness is love. Full stop."

God's Word is clear that man is not fulfilled until he loves God with all of his heart, experiences God's love through the gospel of Jesus Christ, and thereby learns to love others as God does. This is the very nucleus of human life.

Another primary conclusion of the Grant Study was the destructive force of alcohol. The study revealed alcoholism as the single greatest predictor of divorce, depression, and early death. Of course, Don didn't need a seventy-five-year study to tell him that alcoholism played a key role in his relationship with his father.

Papa, Alcohol, and Mixed Memories

It's hard to imagine how the destruction of alcoholism and the power of real love could coexist. Apart from the grace of God, perhaps it can't. For there's no human reason that having grown up with an alcoholic father, Don should have ever deeply loved his dad or been able to gratefully appreciate his strengths. Don had every reason to be bitter or angry. His childhood could have been much happier were it not for the influence of alcohol.

Yet, as a young boy, Don managed to protect his heart from becoming bitter with his father's struggles, while somehow gratefully appreciating his strengths. Earl Sisk Sr., known to his children as "Papa," had been raised by a stepmother who had little affection for him or his brothers. Don seemed to grasp, early on, that his dad grew up with struggles that probably pushed him to the bottle for relief. But despite his alcoholism, Earl was a hard worker with a great mind. He could add numbers in his head quickly and solve nearly any mathematic problem almost instantly.

Don and his dad shared a love of baseball. As a boy, Don was proud that his dad could remember the entire lineup of their favorite major league baseball teams. And nearly every week of the summer, Don and Earl would sit near the radio listening to the great baseball announcer Harry Caray call the St. Louis Cardinals games, both of their vivid imaginations helping paint the scene. At least once a year, Earl would take Don to watch the Cardinals play in St. Louis. In fact, Don and Papa were in the stands in 1947 when the Cardinals played the Brooklyn Dodgers.

At second base that day, for the first time in St. Louis, was the legendary Jackie Robinson in his rookie year. It was a historic moment that Don fondly recalls to this day.

Praying for Papa

When Don came to know Jesus Christ as Saviour, his first thought was, "This is wonderful!" His second thought was, "I wish my dad was saved." He instantly developed a burden to see Papa come to Jesus Christ, for he knew Jesus was the ultimate fulfillment of Earl's emptiness and deepest longings, which alcohol could never fill.

Except for the occasional funeral, Earl never attended church, and Don didn't really know why. He never manifested much of a knowledge of God or displayed concern for his own sin and need for a Saviour. Rather than attend church, the weekends were Earl's time to himself and his friends, given mostly to drinking and being away from his family. He would often come home drunk. Those were horrible days for the Sisk family. Under the influence of alcohol, Earl did and said things that he would never have done otherwise.

From the time Don was saved as a teen and into his early days of marriage, he prayed that God would soften his father's heart toward the gospel. He knew if Papa would trust Jesus, his life would change. Things began to shift while Don was working the foundry and attending Black Oak Baptist Church in Gary, Indiana. Black Oak hosted two revivals each year, in the spring and in the fall. The March 1953 revival brought a guest pastor from Kentucky to preach God's Word. For two weeks, the church family met in homes together to pray for the revival. These "cottage prayer meetings" were new to Don, but he and Virginia were eager to take part. Don was asked to lead the Thursday night prayer meeting in the home of one of the church families, and he asked everyone gathered there to pray for his dad's salvation. Earl's name was added to the many others on a prayer list, and after Don shared some prayer promises from the Bible, the group prayed together. For two weeks, Virginia and Don attended the prayer meetings, and by the middle of the second week he was so burdened for his Papa that he could hardly eat or sleep. All he could think was that his dad was lost and on his way to Hell.

A Praying Son and a Repentant Father

The revival meeting began on Monday night. Don and Virginia had recently moved into the mobile home park where Earl and Beulah also lived, so that morning Don dropped by on his way to work to invite Earl to church. Though he had been praying and believing God, Don was surprised by Earl's quick and open response. His dad told him, "Son, I just said to your mother that if you would come by and take us, we would go to the revival meeting."

Don could hardly believe his ears. His heart filled with hope and anticipation of what God might be doing in Earl's heart. He continued into his workday at the foundry. Though he was making cores all day, his mind and heart were completely engaged in prayer. Rather than eat lunch, Don chose to fast and pray for his father's salvation.

When he got home from work that evening, he related the good news to Virginia. After dinner and preparation for church, they paused again to pray for Earl. Don begged, "Dear Lord, please save my dad. If you would save him I would do anything you would ever ask me to do. I would go any place you want me to go. Please save him. Please let him come to church tonight. Don't let him change his mind."

A few minutes later Don and Virginia pulled the car in front of Papa's mobile home, and to their delight, Earl and Beulah were ready and waiting.

As they arrived at church, Virginia took her in-laws to their seats while Don went straight to the basement of the church for a pre-service men's prayer meeting. Again, Don asked the men to pray for his father, and they prayed fervently together. That night's service was wonderful. The song service was praiseful, and the preacher preached with power, as Don had prayed that he would. So much was riding on this one sermon and this single opportunity for his father to hear the gospel. He recalled later, "If that preacher had just fooled around that night, I would have shot him." Don prayed through the entire message that God would work in Earl's heart.

As the invitation began, several believers went forward to pray. Don stood next to his dad, wondering what Earl was thinking. As the Lord prompted him, Don quietly leaned over and said, "Papa, I've been praying for your salvation for a long time. I would sure love to see you be saved." The risk seemed worth it, and Don was hoping in faith that his Dad was softening.

Immediately Earl looked at his son and said, "Son, I do want to be saved."

With that, he stepped out of his seat, went forward, and trusted Jesus Christ as his personal Saviour. It was one of the greatest moments of Don's entire life—the culmination of many years of prayer and hope. Seeing his alcoholic, coal-mining father kneel in prayer with an altar worker and pray to accept Jesus was simply unforgettable.

The only thing that would have made the moment sweeter was if Don had been able to share the Scriptures and pray personally with his dad. But at that time in his life he had no idea what to do or say to someone who wanted to receive salvation. Seeing his father at the altar that day gave him a personal burden to learn how to lead others to Jesus Christ.

The night was the beginning of a dramatic change in Papa's life. From the time he was saved until he went to Heaven nineteen years later, Don never heard his dad curse again. Earl completely turned away from alcohol and never took another drink. About two weeks after his salvation, Earl and Don were driving together and passed by a tavern on Colfax Avenue called The Stumble Inn. (Don was always amused with the name, and would remark, "If you didn't stumble in, you would probably stumble out.") Earl looked at the cars in the parking lot and saw that his son (Don's brother), Bo, was there. Tears welled up in Earl's eyes and he said to Don, "I don't know why Bo would spend time in a place like that."

Don marveled that God's grace had caused Earl to nearly forget all the weekends he had spent in places just like The Stumble Inn over the years. Don and Earl both began to pray for Bo, and just a few years later, he too trusted Christ as Saviour and experienced a radical life change through the gospel.

In his later years, Papa often related to Don his great regret of not being saved when he was younger. He would say, "I wish we would have had a soulwinning church in our town." For his part, Don could never remember anyone attempting to influence his dad for the Lord during those early days in Nortonville. Perhaps things might have been different for the Sisk family and for Don's childhood had someone tried to share the gospel with them sooner. Nonetheless, Don rejoiced in his father's salvation, however late it may have come.

Don also remembers the unique role his mother played in Earl's salvation. It was the role of patient love. In fact, Don says that while there were many factors leading to his dad's salvation, the greatest was surely a faithful wife who loved him in spite of the many hardships he caused with his drinking. She never gave up on him.

Beulah was saved as a young girl. She was a hard-working, contented lady who never complained, even in the face of poverty and neglect. Although the Sisk home had little in the way of resources, she was diligent to see that the house was clean and that the family received well-prepared food and lots of love. Her godly testimony contributed to and finally culminated in the salvation of the man she so passionately loved.

I'll See You In Heaven

Briefly fast forwarding our story nineteen years, Don and Virginia were finishing up their first furlough in the States and preparing to return to their missions work in Japan. Leaving family again was difficult, especially as Don's father was aging.

As they prepared to say goodbye, Papa pulled Don aside and gently said, "Son, you are going a long ways away, and I'm an old man. If I never see you on this earth again, I will see you in Heaven."

Little did he know how meaningful those words would become. Just a few months later, Don and Virginia's daughter, Renee, studying in the States at the time, called her parents in Japan with the difficult news that Earl Sr. had suffered a heart attack and gone home to Heaven. The news hit hard. Don wept for the loss of his papa, but also for the joy of knowing he would see him again.

More recently, reflecting back on his father's salvation and the great need for the gospel in the world today, Don commented on the importance of maintaining a heart of compassion and soulwinning fervor. He wrote, "Whenever my burden begins to wane, and I lose my zeal for souls, I often pray, 'Dear Lord, give me a burden for these people the way You gave me a burden for my dad.'"

Over many years of praying and faithfully living out the gospel before them, Don eventually had the privilege of seeing every one of his siblings trust Jesus Christ as Saviour. Perhaps these prayerful victories were the seeds that cultivated a much larger, broader, and growing burden for the families of others across the globe that God would use Don Sisk to reach with the gospel.

Six

THE LORD CALLED

1954–1956

The words from God were simply terrifying to a young Jeremiah: *"Before I formed thee in the belly I knew thee; and before thou camest forth out of the womb I sanctified thee, and I ordained thee a prophet unto the nations"* (Jeremiah 1:5). When Jeremiah heard God's call, he was sure he was "the wrong guy." With paralyzing fear of what this call would mean, he argued, declaring his inability and youth. God's call was completely disruptive of Jeremiah's plans and intentions in life, yet God empowered and enabled him to serve him for over forty years at a pivotal time in Israel's history.

Anyone who grows in grace as a follower of Jesus Christ can expect His disruptive call to eventually become impossible to ignore. This was the case with Don Sisk. From the time he was saved, the Lord was preparing and forming him for a ministry and a destiny that were as unique as Don himself.

A Growing Call

The story of Don's call to ministry is as simple as the word "delight." The more Don delighted himself in the Lord, the more God began to shape in him a new set of desires and then fulfill those desires one day at a time. His call was more a process of growth than a single moment. It was something that God grew within him and which Don increasingly wanted to follow.

It began with a slowly growing desire to preach, while Don was still a teenager. In high school, Don would walk Virginia home after the church services in Nortonville, and then he would catch a ride home to Mannington. On his way home he would think back through the message he had heard in church, replaying it in his mind. He would try to imagine what it would be like to stand behind that sturdy, old pulpit, declaring the truths of the Bible.

To Don, these imagining exercises didn't even qualify as a dream, because dreams have a chance of coming true. This was more of a fantasy or a whim, because Don never imagined for a moment that God would call him—Don Sisk—to preach the Bible.

Every day Don was drawing closer to the Lord, and in turn the Lord was drawing closer to him. The years he worked in the foundry proved to be a strengthening time in his walk with God. He poured into his Bible with a hunger to learn, and in response to his earnest seeking, God increasingly burdened his heart about the matter of preaching. Don would push the burden away, feeling it was impossible that God would want him to preach. But no matter what he did, the burden returned with greater intensity. God's call was becoming more inescapable with every passing day.

God was not only working in Don's heart, but He was also wonderfully working in other members of the Black Oak Baptist Church as well. It seemed that every few weeks another man went forward and humbly said, "I believe God has called me to preach." Naturally, every time another person answered the call to preach, Don would rejoice and feel as though the need for preachers was being met.

The Grace of the Call

Though Don continued to push back, he could not escape the growing knowledge that God was specifically calling him to preach. Little by little, the call became more prominent until he could no longer ignore it. He finally came to a point where he knew that anything less than full surrender would be disobedience. On Thanksgiving Day of 1954 he finally yielded completely: "Here am I, Lord. Send me."

With unbelief and fear clouding his vision, Don went forward at the end of the next church service to make his decision public. He told Pastor Jones, "I believe God wants me to preach." The pastor directed Don to an older man, and the two prayed together. Afterward, Don felt compelled to express how fearful he was of God's call to preach. He said, "While I believe God has called me to preach, I don't know how in the world I'll ever be a preacher."

"How did you get saved?" the man nudged.

"I got saved by the grace of God."

"Well, if you're going to be a preacher, you'll have to do that by the grace of God, too."

This was a defining moment in Don's life. The statement made by the Apostle Paul, "…by the grace of God I am what I am" (1 Corinthians 15:10) became Don's personal motto. He realized that whatever the Lord allowed him to do, it would be done only by His amazing grace.

Sharing the Call Together

Through all of this time, God was equally working in Virginia's heart regarding their call. Her heart was also becoming more tender to doing God's will together.

As Don made his call public, Virginia recognized her role as a wife to support and complete Don in whatever God called him to do. She saw Don's call as a call for both of them—a life work and vision they would share. She would be her husband's companion in ministry.

Just two weeks after Don made the public commitment to be a preacher, Virginia went forward after a Sunday morning message to make a public statement before the church family: "Since God has called Don to be a preacher, I want to be the very best wife that I can possibly be." From that moment, the Sisks were both fully surrendered and dedicated to follow the Lord wherever He would lead.

Virginia's decision would prove as essential to their call as Don's, for without a godly wife to labor beside and support him, Don would never have seen God do all that He has done in their lives and ministry. From their earliest days together, Virginia has been a gracious, servant-hearted, hard-working lady who loves her husband, her family, and the people they've served in ministry all over the world.

Virginia chose to be content with whatever blessings God would choose to give them, and she dedicated herself to making their home a delightful, loving, and grace-filled place. In every place they lived together—and they have been many and varied—she accepted the conditions and labored to make them neat, clean, and welcoming. Don took comfort in knowing that every day as he returned from work and ministry, he would be greeted by a godly woman who, with great discipline, kept their home in order.

Spending quality time together was a priority for the Sisks. Every Friday they would take their budgeted ten dollars to the market to buy groceries together. Their date almost always continued at White Castle, where they could buy six hamburgers, two cokes, and an order of fries to share for less than a dollar. Don and Virginia learned in the early stages in their marriage to make the most out of their time together, regardless how much money they had. God would later use this spirit of contentment to stabilize their hearts during difficult and unpredictable financial seasons.

A Growing Family

One of the greatest days of Don and Virginia's early marriage was the day they learned that Virginia was expecting. They waited through those expectant months with great anticipation of the birth of their first child. This was long before ultrasounds, so they would not learn the gender of their baby until birth.

Finally, the day arrived—November 24, 1953. Don escorted his wife into the labor room at Methodist Hospital in Gary, Indiana, then paced the waiting room in nervous anticipation.

After what seemed like forever, the doctor stepped into the waiting room and announced, "Mr. Sisk, it's a girl!" The young couple were completely overwhelmed with the goodness of God as they held their precious baby, Angela Renee, and thanked God for the wonderful gift He had given them.

Angela—or Renee, as she has been called most of her life—was a beautiful girl. Like most first-time parents, the Sisks were sure Renee was "gifted" in almost every area. In a short time, she was talking and walking and growing rapidly.

Soon after, God provided an opportunity for the family to move into a slightly larger trailer, which their baby girl filled with laughter. Don and Virginia were grateful parents who reveled in every moment they shared as a family.

Big Changes, Big Responsibilities

In late 1954, Don was only twenty-one years old, but two major life events had already impacted him—he had yielded to God's call to preach, and he had become a parent. Both events brought radical, immediate, and permanent change. And with these changes, God's hand was obviously moving circumstances in ways that he could not control or explain. Don claimed the promise of Proverbs 3:6, *"In all thy ways acknowledge him, and he shall direct thy paths."* As he did so, God fulfilled His promise and began to clearly direct his family's path.

A few months after his call to preach, Don went to visit his sister. She had told her neighbors that her brother was a preacher, and that he was coming to visit. During Don's visit, one of those neighbors dropped by unannounced to ask, "Where is the man of God?"

That was the first time Don saw himself through the eyes of others, and at that moment he suddenly realized things would never be the same. He knew the world would forever look at him as a preacher, and with that came great responsibility.

Change is a necessary aspect of growth, and during this season the Sisks were experiencing changes that led them into unfamiliar territory. By God's grace, Don wanted to be the best preacher he could be, so he felt he should further his education. With little knowledge of what lay ahead, they began to seek the Lord's guidance regarding Bible college.

They were fearful that in themselves they were inadequate, yet they were confident in God's grace and secure in His call. They knew He would lead, enable, and provide for the very call they sought to obey.

Deciding which college to attend proved to be a big task. In time, the Lord led Don to move the family back to Kentucky to a small college just a short distance from Nortonville called Bethel Baptist College. God gave Don peace that this was a place where he would receive a biblically-based education, so Don enrolled to begin classes in the winter of 1955.

In preparation for the move, Don partnered with his brother-in-law to purchase a service station, which would serve as his primary source of income for the coming months. Then Don and his family packed their belongings into their 1951 Pontiac and returned to Nortonville. The little mobile home that held such precious memories of their first years together was left for Don's parents to live in.

One day at a time, details began to fall into place. God used the service station to provide an adequate income—enough to support a family and pay for Bible college. The family rented a small house on Main Street and even had money left over to buy a few pieces of furniture. God's provision and guidance in all of these areas kept bringing Romans 11:29 to their minds: *"For the gifts and calling of God are without repentance."* This verse became increasingly meaningful to them as they watched God unfold their future and provide every step of the journey.

A Humbling Opportunity

God's call is not eventual; it is now. His will is not someday; it is today. This principle caught Don off guard. He saw preaching and serving as something he was preparing to do in the future, not as something God wanted him to do immediately. Yet, God's call often means obeying and being useful to God right now—even as we are preparing for "eventually."

The Sisks quickly settled into their new home amid familiar surroundings and began attending the Nortonville Baptist Church. One Sunday afternoon between church services, there was a knock on their front door. Don opened the door to see the expectant faces of four men he did not know. One of the men explained who they were: "We're from the Johnston's Island Baptist Church. May we speak with you for a moment?"

Don invited the men into his home where they shared their story—and their request. Their church had no pastor, and they had been praying for God to raise up a godly man who would serve in that role.

The missions director of Nortonville Baptist Church, R. W. Gass, heard of their need and recommended Don. The men asked if he would pray about serving as the new pastor of Johnston's Island Baptist.

Don and Virginia were speechless. Although he was certain God had called him to preach, the title of "pastor" seemed beyond him—a role of which he could never be worthy. Yet, he was absolutely positive God had called him to preach, and he had already decided to never turn down an opportunity to share God's Word with others.

The pause of that moment is forever etched into Don's mind and heart. The men continued, "We would like to invite you to come preach for our church next Sunday as a pastoral candidate. Will you come?"

Graciously, humbly, and fearfully, Don accepted the invitation. Immediately he began to be anxious about that next church service. Less than seven days away, it loomed in his mind every waking moment. Up to that point, Don had little experience preaching in a church setting. Most of his preaching opportunities had been at prayer services, in jails, and on street corners.

The first and only opportunity Don had ever had to preach in a church setting had been at State Street Baptist Church in Hammond, Indiana. On that Sunday morning Don, Virginia, and Renee headed to Hammond to fill the pulpit both Sunday morning and Sunday night. It was his first time preaching in a real church service, and he relished every moment of it. After the service, a man handed him an envelope and said, "Mr. Sisk, this is your honorarium. We really appreciate you coming to preach for us."

Inside the envelope was a check for twenty-five dollars. Don thought, "I'm not supposed to be paid for preaching!" Feeling unsettled about receiving money for something he enjoyed so much, he gave the money to his pastor, Pastor Jones.

This memory replayed in Don's mind as the Sisk family drove to the Johnston's Island Baptist Church the Sunday after the men visited his

SIX—THE LORD CALLED

home. The directions they received led them to a small church with no sign. As he got out of the car and introduced himself, no one seemed to know who he was. It didn't take long to discover he was at the Cumberland Presbyterian Church. The members redirected him, and a few moments later, the Sisks arrived at Johnston's Island, nervous but eager.

That day Don preached with the passion that had consumed his life since the day he accepted Jesus. He enjoyed the opportunity, but he couldn't imagine that the church would actually want him to be their pastor.

Just a few days later, Don received a phone call from one of the men who had first visited his home: "Pastor Sisk, our church has voted for you to become our pastor." The news was exciting and jolting all at the same time. Fear once again fell upon Don's heart as the devil tried to tell him that such a position was too high for him. Through a short season of prayer, the Lord affirmed to Don and Virginia that this was indeed His will, and Don chose to trust that God was bigger than his inhibitions and inabilities. With a courage that only the inadequate can know, Don called the man back to share his decision: "I know very little about being a pastor, but if you will have me, I would be glad to accept the position."

And so, with dependence upon the Lord's abundant grace, Don set out on yet another adventure—pastoring a local church. He began his pastorate at Johnston's Island Baptist Church the second Sunday in January 1956. This church, like many other rural churches in these days, had Sunday school every week but preaching services only twice a month. This enabled rural pastors to serve multiple congregations. Don was a clean vessel, and the Lord delighted in using him.

Just two weeks prior to beginning his service as pastor at Johnston's Island, Don had filled the pulpit as a guest preacher for the New Year's Eve service at Richland Baptist Church in Richland, Kentucky. After the service, Don was approached by a couple he did not know.

The couple introduced themselves as Mr. and Mrs. Kirkwood and got immediately to their question: "We are members of the Silent Run Baptist Church, and we don't have a pastor. Will you preach for us this Sunday?"

Don was in awe that God was so quickly opening doors for him to share God's Word. He jumped at the chance to preach God's Word on his "free Sunday" and accepted the invitation. So, before he had even begun his pastorate at Johnston's Island, Don was headed to Silent Run to preach the first Sunday of January, 1956. There his family was greeted by about fifty gracious people, and they enjoyed a wonderful Lord's Day together.

The very next week, the Kirkwoods called with an unexpected announcement: the congregation of Silent Run had voted unanimously for Don to become their pastor. Don was just getting used to the idea of being a pastor of *one* church, and now he was being asked to serve *two* congregations. The idea of pastoring two churches had never occurred to him. Most men would have considered this an impossible task, but Don believed God's hand was in these open doors and that God could do the impossible.

So in January of 1955, Don was a young husband and father in Bible college, working at a service station, and pastoring two rural churches in western Kentucky, not far from where he'd grown up. He preached at Johnston's Island Baptist Church the second and fourth Sundays of each month and at Silent Run Baptist Church the first and third Sundays. It was a busy but exciting season for the Sisk family.

I've Never Seen This Before

It wasn't long before Don and his brother-in-law sold their service station to a family member. Don continued to work at the station on the weekends, but he wanted to focus more on pastoring and pursuing his education. He was twenty-two years old as he began to pastor, and Virginia was nineteen. They were nearly the youngest people in both churches, but the church families were gracious and kind and treated them as their own children. It was a wonderful growing and learning experience.

While the members of each church were growing spiritually, there was very little numerical growth. Don recalls baptizing only two people at Johnston's Island during his first year. He had never seen it done differently, but that was about to change. During a revival at Silent Run, Don learned a truth that would give him a new and lifelong perspective on ministry and outreach.

Pastor David Brown, Don's pastor in Nortonville, preached the first revival meeting at Silent Run. After that Monday night service he said, "I'll get down here tomorrow afternoon at 1:00 so we can make some visits before church."

Though Don was unfamiliar with the idea of "visiting people," he thought it sounded great and was eager to spend some time learning from his own pastor. Up to this point he had never heard the term "soulwinning" and had never personally seen someone accept the Lord outside of a church setting. In his mind, an unsaved person needed to attend church, hear preaching, experience conviction, go forward during the invitation, and learn how to be saved from a trained worker. This was the only way he had ever seen it happen.

The next day, Don and Pastor Brown spent the afternoon visiting people and inviting them to the revival. During their visit with a man named Ruby Jackson, Pastor Brown asked Ruby a simple question that was entirely new to Don: "Sir, do you know for sure that you are saved and going to Heaven?"

Ruby did not hesitate. "Oh no, I'm not saved. If I were to die today I'm sure I wouldn't go to Heaven."

Pastor Brown asked if he would like to know how to be saved and have a home in Heaven. Ruby responded with interest.

At this point, Don expected Pastor Brown to tell Ruby to come to church that night to hear how to be saved, but instead, Pastor Brown opened his Bible and began sharing the gospel from the Romans Road: "*For all have sinned, and come short of the glory of God...*" (Romans 3:23), "*For the wages of sin is death...*" (Romans 6:23), "*For whosoever shall call upon the name of the Lord shall be saved...*" (Romans 10:13). Ruby listened carefully, and Don couldn't believe what he was seeing.

All through the gospel presentation, Don expected Pastor Brown to stop at some point and tell Ruby to come to church that night if he wanted to accept Jesus Christ as his Saviour. But Pastor Brown went through the entire plan of salvation right there in Ruby's living room. Then he said, "Ruby, I'm going to pray, and while I am praying I invite you to pray. If you really mean it, I encourage you to ask Jesus to be your Saviour."

To Don's amazement, right there in the middle of the afternoon and nowhere near a church, all three men got on their knees and prayed. Don still wasn't sure what was going on or if this was acceptable. After the prayer, Pastor Brown said, "Ruby, did you ask Jesus Christ to become your Saviour?"

"Yes, I did."

Pastor Brown continued, "The Bible says that if you ask Him, He will save you: 'For whosoever shall call upon the name of the Lord shall be saved.' So Ruby, are you saved?"

Ruby smiled, "Oh yes, I'm saved."

Don was filled with wonder and amazement as he looked at Ruby and saw once-empty eyes filled with the joy and presence of the Lord.

But the visit at Ruby's house wasn't over!

Ruby's son, Bobby, was sitting beside his dad during the visit, and after they all prayed, the boy said, "I need to do that, too." Once again, Pastor Brown went through the Bible, this time showing Bobby how to be saved. And once again, the men knelt as Bobby asked Christ to be his Saviour.

At church that evening, Don awkwardly stood before the pre-service men's prayer meeting, unsure how to share what had happened. "I've never seen this before," he told them. "But this afternoon, as Pastor Brown and I were out visiting, Ruby Jackson and his son Bobby were both saved in their home."

The men immediately rejoiced, and one said, "Ruby Jackson got saved? I can't believe that! I work with Ruby. He cusses every other word."

Yet it was true! The Holy Spirit had worked in a miraculous way in the lives of Ruby and Bobby. In fact, they attended service that night and publicly professed their faith in Jesus as Saviour.

Several others were saved during the revival meeting that week, and Don was able to baptize a few new Christians when the meetings were over. Seeing Ruby and Bobby saved in their home made a lasting impression on him. He never looked at a soul the same way again, and he never lost the desire to share the gospel personally with anyone who would listen.

Not long after this experience, God burdened Don's heart for a lady named Miss Edmonson who attended Sunday school regularly, but never stayed for church. With the memory of Pastor Brown and the visit to Ruby's fresh in his mind, Don decided to visit this lady and share the same verses that Pastor Brown used. He had marked them in his Bible that afternoon and was eager to share them with others. With fear and anticipation, he headed to Miss Edmondson's house to show her how to be saved.

En route, the devil worked to discourage him. "This is not a good idea," Don thought to himself, "I don't know what I'm doing. This won't work. I might mess it up." He pushed the thoughts aside and pressed on. Even as he arrived at the home, however, he was nervous. By the time he knocked on the front door, he secretly hoped she would not be home.

If it didn't happen to him personally, Don wouldn't have believed what happened next. Miss Edmondson answered the door and said,

"Pastor Sisk, I am so glad to see you. I've just been listening to Pastor Utley preach on the radio and I believe I need to be saved. Can you help me?"

In absolute amazement, Don asked Miss Edmondson and her daughter to sit on the porch where he opened his Bible and went through the gospel. A short time later, they both accepted Jesus Christ as their personal Saviour. The Lord had orchestrated a divine meeting that day, and Don celebrated the fact that he had obeyed the Holy Spirit's prompting in spite of his fear and hesitation. How differently that day might have gone had he given into his fears!

A Passion that Shaped a Life

Over the decades, Don has often observed, "Soulwinning is better caught than taught." He never forgot "catching it" as he sat that afternoon with Pastor Brown and watched two men accept Jesus Christ as Saviour. Since then, Don has never gotten over the sacred delight of helping others understand the gospel and trust Jesus.

Consider it for a moment: On a seemingly random Tuesday afternoon, one seasoned pastor took another young pastor out to make a few visits. That day two souls passed from death to life, from condemnation to justification. And that day, one young pastor caught a lifetime passion to win others to Jesus Christ. The fruit from that afternoon visit—and another made shortly after—continues to abound to this day in the hearts of thousands of souls around the world.

Seven

THE LORD DEVELOPED

1956–1962

The intricacy of putting together your own future would be overwhelming apart from knowing and loving God. There is wonderful comfort found in discovering that He knows the path, He controls the circumstances, He promises to give direction, and He has an eternal purpose. Proverbs 3:5–6 promises, *"Trust in the LORD with all thine heart; and lean not unto thine own understanding. In all thy ways acknowledge him, and he shall direct thy paths."*

From their earliest days of marriage and ministry together, Don and Virginia made it their habit to trust in the Lord and acknowledge Him in all their ways. They knew that apart from God and His will, they were destined to look back with regrets.

So they practiced the simple discipline of acknowledging Him with the intent to obey. They determined that Jesus was their Lord, and they would follow Him wherever and however He led. In every decision, they sought His will. They were surrendered before they knew the plan or the outcomes. They simply trusted that God knew best how to use them, bless them, and fulfill their deepest desires.

Along the way, God was at work enlarging their hearts, family, vision, ministry experience, education, influence, and opportunities—in wonderful ways beyond their control. As a husband, father, and pastor of two churches, Don found juggling his responsibilities quite a task at times. After two years at Bethel Baptist College and completing the program offered, he began classes at Murray State University from which he graduated two years later. While attending Murray State, Don was driving sixty miles three days a week for classes and pastoring two churches.

Because both churches were small, the Sisk's primary source of income was Don's secular job. He worked in the service station and after finishing college, began teaching at a junior high school. He taught English, science, and math and grew to love his students immensely.

It had been two years since Don had taken on the role of pastoring two churches. Silent Run was beginning to grow rather quickly. Don was eager to see the church not only expand in size but also in spiritual growth. He encouraged the people to have services every Sunday, rather than just every other week. Habits are difficult to break, but eventually the church warmed to the idea and voted to have weekly services. With the people of Silent Run needing his full attention, Don resigned as the pastor of Johnston's Island.

A Growing Ministry

Just two and half years later, the Lord brought another unexpected transition into Don's life. He was preaching a revival meeting at the Second Baptist Church in Providence, Kentucky, a tiny town with about three thousand residents. He and Virginia picked up a lady for the revival services, and as she got in the car she said, "Pastor Sisk, did you hear that Pastor Crowel has resigned from the Second Baptist Church?" The very moment she said that, God spoke directly to Don's heart: "This is the church I want you to pastor." Don kept this leading in his heart and waited on God, curious to see how the Lord planned to develop these circumstances.

Three weeks passed, and Don was on his front porch swing in blue jeans and an old t-shirt with his daughter Renee. Like every rural home in the area, the Sisks' yard was dotted with free-range chickens and a large garden nearby.

A car pulled up and parked in the driveway, and Don recognized the three men walking toward the house from the revival services at Second Baptist. One of the three explained their visit: "We are the pulpit committee from Second Baptist Church in Providence. Pastor Sisk, we've been praying about it, and a good number of people think perhaps you should become our new pastor. Would you come and preach as a candidate for pastor?"

Don marveled at how the Lord had prepared him for this moment. There was no denying God's leading. Nothing these men said came as a surprise.

In those days, it wasn't uncommon for revival services to last two weeks, so Don had already preached fourteen messages at this church. Half-kidding, he asked the men if they were sure they needed to hear him again before voting on him as a candidate. The committee was confident of the outcome, but they still set a date for Don to preach one more time before the church voted on him as their new pastor.

Some days later, after preaching his fifteenth sermon at Second Baptist Church, Don received a call asking him to become the new pastor. Don knew without a single doubt this was the sovereign hand of God at work in his life and accepted immediately. With the new position came another move. The Sisks moved from their country home to Providence into the parsonage near the church. Their new home needed repairs, but with a little paint and special attention from Virginia, it became beautiful. The house was one block away from Second Baptist Church, so Don enjoyed the convenience of being able to walk to church whenever he needed.

This was Don's first full-time pastorate. The church paid him enough to be able to provide for his family, so for the first time since entering the ministry, Don could fully devote himself to pastoring.

These were exciting days. He spent countless hours in prayer and Bible study as he worked to spiritually feed his new congregation.

A New Addition to the Family

During their second year serving at Providence, the Sisks were thrilled to discover that another baby was on the way. Some months later Don once again found himself in a waiting room as Virginia delivered their second child—this time a boy, who they named Timothy. Don was ecstatic at the thought of raising a son for the Lord.

Renee and Timothy were just over seven years apart. No two children are alike, and the Sisks learned this firsthand. Both children grew up to be different and unique in their own way, yet both were a tremendous blessing to their parents.

A Hunger for Bible Doctrine

Don's two years at Bethel Baptist College had been profitable, but he yearned to know more about the Bible. He had taken classes such as Homiletics, Life of Christ, the Life and Letters of Paul, and several other Bible courses, but he still felt he was lacking needed knowledge of God's Word. He spent several hours a day studying the Bible, gleaning as much as he could to serve God's people.

Pastor David Brown, the man who had been instrumental in teaching Don about soulwinning, introduced him to many good books that Don dove into with great hunger. Some of the books Don found difficult to understand. For instance, he struggled through *Strong's Systematic Theology*. He originally bought the three-book set because of its name—Strong. Don wanted to be strong in the Word of God so the books seemed like a perfect fit. Not being a man to quit or take the easy way out, Don read through each book with a dictionary and Bible dictionary close at hand. The more he studied, the more he considered going to seminary.

At the time Don was a Southern Baptist. The natural decision for him would have been to attend the nearby Southern Baptist Seminary in Louisville, Kentucky. However, in the late '50s and '60s, this school had liberal leanings. There were teachers on staff who did not believe the first eleven chapters of Genesis were actually God's Word, questioned the virgin birth of Christ, and denied the inspiration of Scripture. Don watched others leave to attend this seminary only to return with their faith destroyed. Under no circumstance was Don going to study where the whole of the Bible was not believed and preached.

Don's strong personal stand with his church for biblical doctrine cost him some friendships, but he never regretted standing for biblical truth when many were attempting to dilute critical doctrines of the Christian faith.

Untold Millions

In the midst of these pressing issues Don traveled to Louisville, Kentucky, to attend an evangelistic conference at Broadway Baptist Church. Dr. Baker Cauthen, head of the foreign mission board of the Southern Baptist Convention, was the keynote speaker, and his message on "The Untold Millions" deeply touched Don's heart. At first he thought God was telling him to get the church more involved in missions through prayer and giving. Then he realized not only was God talking to him about leading the church to do more for missions, but He was speaking to his heart about going to the mission field himself.

With the call of missions on his heart that night, Don exited quickly in hopes of getting alone with God. When he reached his hotel room, he went to the bathroom with his Bible and locked the door. He cried out to God and said, "I believe You want me to be a missionary, but I don't know how in the world I could do that. I can't go to Louisville Seminary."

Southern Baptists require their missionaries to attend their seminaries, and Don knew he could not go to any of the schools offered. He felt he was at a dead end, but in a spirit of humility he prayed, "Dear Lord, I don't know how I can get to the mission field, but if You will open the doors and show me the way, I will go anywhere You lead me."

The next day, he returned to Providence and continued pastoring. He spoke with Virginia about the burden the Lord had given him for the mission field. He wrote the Southern Baptist Convention asking for their insight, but they assured Don he was doing a good job where he was. Actually, in addition to Don's doctrinal concerns regarding seminary, there was another reason he was at a dead end to serve as a Southern Baptist missionary: his age. Southern Baptist missionaries could not be sent to the field after age thirty-three (for concerns that they would be too old to learn a new language and adapt to a new culture). Although Don was just twenty-nine, he didn't have enough years left to attend seminary, receive training, raise support, and get to the field before the cut-off.

That year, Don received an award for pastoring one of the top ten Southern Baptist churches in Kentucky. He had baptized over fifty people that year, and God was blessing the church. In the midst of it all, Don found himself longing for something more—the mission field. He simply could not escape the burden that God had placed upon his heart.

A Providential Relationship

Not long after, Don began hearing about several independent Baptist mission boards. One in particular caught his attention: Baptist International Missions, Incorporated (BIMI) in Chattanooga, Tennessee. This was a new mission board, just recently organized.

Don discovered that Dr. Freeny, the general director of BIMI, would be preaching in a church not far from Providence. So without telling anyone but Virginia, Don drove forty miles to one of the only independent Baptist churches in the area to hear this man preach.

That night Dr. Freeny preached on missions, and after the service, Don had the opportunity to share his burden. Dr. Freeny graciously offered to come to the Sisks' home and talk to them about missions, and Don eagerly accepted his offer.

Days later, Dr. Freeny sat in the Sisks' living room and showed slides of South America, the Bahamas, Nicaragua, and other foreign fields. Even with the pictures of so many countries desperately needing the gospel flashing on the wall, Don knew that God had clearly burdened his heart for one place—Japan.

Since the day God began dealing with Don about missions it seemed everywhere he looked he saw or heard something about Japan. Then, too, there was a news account that Don had read as a twelve-year-old boy that suddenly burned fresh in his memory. The article, written just after World War II, related that in Japan the Emperor Hirohito had been worshipped as a god. But when Japan was defeated, the Emperor came before the people and told them he was not a god after all. That day, the spiritual hope of millions of Japanese crumbled to the ground.

Even as an unsaved twelve year old, Don was saddened by the story. "What do people do when they worship someone as god, and all of a sudden he tells them he is not god?" he wondered. And now as an adult, in light of his current burden for missions, thoughts of the hopeless people in Japan consumed him.

The fellowship with Dr. Freeny was refreshing. He believed that God was indeed calling Don to the mission field. They prayed together, and although the Sisks did not see him again for some time, his vote of confidence encouraged them greatly.

"What Would Keep You from Coming?"

Some months later, the Lord revealed yet another concern about the direction of the Southern Baptist convention. Don asked a few questions about the money the church had given for missions and was distressed to learn that only between ten and fifteen percent of the money given was actually applied to foreign missions. The rest was used for administrative costs in the States. This was distressing news, and the percentages seemed greatly imbalanced to Don.

With a desire to provoke change, Don wrote an article about the situation that was published in the Kentucky state *Western Recorder,* which was circulated among every Southern Baptist church in the state and among the missionaries who had studied at Louisville Seminary. In the article, Don questioned why money given specifically for missions was being used otherwise. He laid out the facts in an effort to inform others of what he believed was a great misuse of funds.

Of all the missionaries who had received the paper, the first to respond was a missionary from Japan named Don Mobley. He and his wife were serving in Akita-ken, a large area in northern Japan with a population of 3.5 million people.

In his letter, Mr. Mobley wrote, "Don, I don't know anything about you. I don't know your age or educational background, but when I read the article, I was certain of your heart for missions."

His next question would change Don's life: "What would keep you from coming to Japan?"

With that single question, what had once been a burden for Japan suddenly became an open door. Still in shock, Don showed the letter to Virginia. He read the letter to the church and asked the church family to pray for him.

A Transforming Moment

About this time Pastor David Brown began to pastor an independent Baptist church in Harvey, Illinois. He invited Don to come preach for a revival meeting—Don's first time to preach in an independent Baptist church. After preaching and fellowshipping with the people, he came to find that they were not all that different from the Southern Baptist churches he knew. The doctrine was the same as what he preached at Providence.

Soon after, Pastor Brown invited the Sisks to stay at their home and attend The Sword of the Lord Conference. The idea of a short family vacation was appealing, and the Sisks readily accepted the offer.

The first night of the conference could not have been more exciting. The Sisks enjoyed the preaching of Dr. Tom Malone, Dr. Bob Jones, Jr., Dr. Jack Hyles, Dr. John R. Rice, and several others. Don was blown away by the passionate preaching of these men and their vision for the ministry of the gospel. By Wednesday morning of the conference, Don told Virginia, "I have no idea what these people are, but whatever they are, that's what we are!"

At the conference, Dr. Jack Hyles preached a sermon entitled "Let's Go Soulwinning." This sermon had a tremendous impact on Don. The meeting ended late Friday night, and the Sisks began their eight-hour drive home to Kentucky. When they arrived, it was now Saturday morning, and Don had the sudden desire to go soulwinning. Names of people who needed the Lord started quickly coming to mind.

God led Don to visit an elderly couple named Mr. and Mrs. Hibbs, and to Don's great delight, they both accepted Jesus Christ as Saviour. Later in the day another man came to Christ, and Don was greatly encouraged by the power of the gospel and what God was doing in his own heart.

The next morning Don stood to make announcements in the church service, as he normally did, when God's Spirit said, "Just preach." And so he did—for well over an hour. It was an unbelievable service. Many people were saved, and many others were deeply convicted. The church service lasted nearly forty-five minutes longer than normal, but the people left rejoicing that God had met with them.

There was quite a stir the next day as people in the little town of Providence heard what happened at Second Baptist Church. Some thought Don had gone crazy. In reality, it was one of the conference messages by John R. Rice that had made such a difference. It was the first message Don had ever heard on the fullness of the Spirit. After hearing that sermon, he cried out to God, "I don't understand all of it, but I want everything You have for me and I want to give my entire self to You." That moment changed his life and ministry.

With a peace and courage he had never experienced, Don continued serving in Providence while awaiting the Lord's direction. There was a sweet peace in the Sisk home after the Sword of the Lord Conference. Don and Virginia's relationship was flourishing more than it ever had before, and God was at work in both of their hearts in powerful and transforming ways.

Eight
THE LORD PREPARED

1963–1964

Serving the Lord at Providence was exciting. There was no doubt God was blessing this church as many people were trusting Christ and being added to the church. But despite the blessings, Don felt in his spirit that the Lord had something different in store for his future, and he continued prayerfully seeking God's will about the call to missions. His passion to bring the lost to Jesus Christ was growing daily.

Unfolding Opportunities

In 1963, the second largest church in the regional Southern Baptist Convention Association lost their pastor. The pulpit committee came to hear Don preach on two separate occasions and spoke with him about the possibility of pastoring their church. They were ready to call Don to be their pastor if he was willing.

The offer represented a great opportunity, but the more Don prayed, the more he knew God wanted him to serve outside of the Southern Baptist Convention. He turned down the opportunity, wondering what was next. A few days later, Don received a call from his friend, Pastor Dave Brown, who needed an associate pastor. The church was looking for someone who could direct the outreach program and teach soulwinning in the church's Bible college and church. He asked Don to pray about it, assuring him that the church would welcome him into the position if Don felt God's leading to come.

Calvary Baptist Church was located in Harvey, Illinois, and was about the same size as the church in Providence. Don knew in his heart that within a short time he would be on the mission field, so the opportunity to be an associate pastor seemed perfect. He could prepare for missions, serve a church family, and wait until God made His timing clear. After much prayer, Don accepted the position.

Spiritual Resistance

During a time of faith-filled transition, Satan always brings testing and resistance. On the Sisks' first weekend in Harvey, it was almost as if Satan silently said, "Oh, no you don't!"

The family arrived in Harvey late on a Saturday evening, tired and drained from the move. Their possessions were well packed in a U-Haul trailer, and the family arrived in their car. It was late, so they stayed the night with the Browns. That night, temperatures dropped and the morning brought an icy freeze. The car was so frozen over that the Sisks couldn't retrieve their clothes for their first Sunday at Calvary Baptist Church. The Browns loaned them enough clothing to "look halfway decent for church" but this certainly wasn't how they had envisioned their first Sunday!

The frustration and embarrassment of that first day soon faded, and God began to bless their ministry at Calvary Baptist. Don was grateful for the time he was able to spend soulwinning and mentoring others in gospel ministry. Nearly every week, the Sisks personally brought people they had led to Christ during the week down the aisle to be baptized. They enjoyed every minute of this season of ministry.

A Soulwinning Story

Don never got over the joy of personally sharing the gospel of Jesus Christ with others. In fact, the longer He served Jesus, the greater this passion grew. One particular soulwinning experience stands out in Don's mind from his time at Calvary Baptist.

He was knocking doors one evening with a Christian friend, Richard Griffin. They arrived at a brand new house and saw a man, his wife, and their two girls sitting outside in their yard. Don approached the yard, introduced himself, and began talking with them. The man's name was Perry, and his wife's name was Mary. When Don asked if they went to church and if they were saved, the answer to both questions was "no."

With their permission, Don began to tell them how they could know Jesus as their Saviour. They listened intently to every word of the gospel, yet never showed any emotion. When Don talked about being sinners deserving of Hell, they nodded their heads in agreement. After sharing the entire gospel message, Don asked if they believed Jesus died for them, and if they wanted to accept His free gift of salvation. Still, without any emotion, they both answered "yes."

The couple bowed their heads with Don and asked the Lord Jesus to save them. Don gave them verses on assurance and asked if he could pick them up for church on Sunday. Perry insisted they could drive themselves, and he promised Don they would be there.

Don and Richard left the house bewildered. While they rejoiced in the couple's profession to accept Christ, their lack of emotion made Don and Richard wonder if it was a true conversion. They prayed together that the family would attend church and continued with their visits.

Sunday arrived, and right before Sunday school, Perry, Mary, and their two daughters stepped out of their car, dressed and ready for services. Don was delighted! After Sunday school, he invited them to come forward during the invitation to tell the church family of their decision to trust Christ. After the message that morning, Perry and Mary walked the aisle to follow in believer's baptism.

After church, Perry had questions for Don about the message the pastor had preached on giving. Don took a Bible and began to disciple Perry in the principles of biblical stewardship. Perry's heart was receptive, and the next week the whole family came to church with their offerings. It was amazing to see God's Holy Spirit at work in this new Christian family.

From that day forward, Perry and Mary were some of the most faithful members of Calvary Baptist Church. They attended every service and became wholeheartedly involved. Eventually, Mary became the organist and Perry served as a deacon. Both of their daughters grew up at Calvary, attended and graduated from a Christian college, and married godly Christian men.

Don learned to trust the Holy Spirit's work in the hearts of others—even when that work wasn't immediately apparent through outward signs of emotion.

An Inescapable Call

Serving at Calvary Baptist, under the tremendous preaching of Pastor Brown, gave Don many opportunities and experiences for growth. Twice each month Don preached in the church. The Brown and Sisk families became close friends. Their children played together, and the fellowship the families shared was a true gift from God. It would have been easy for the Sisks to stay in Harvey for the rest of their lives. Yet, as much as Don enjoyed ministry at Calvary Baptist, with every passing day, his desire for the mission field grew. He let the church know that his time with them was short term, because God would soon take them to the mission field.

One Saturday, as Don was soulwinning, his burden for missions was heavy on his heart. Unsure what to do next, he simply prayed, "Lord, I'm not sure when you want me to move forward on my plans to go to the mission field, but tomorrow in church, if either Virginia or Renee go forward during the invitation, I will see this as a sign that you want me to publicly take the next step."

The next morning, Pastor Brown preached and gave such a general invitation that nearly everyone in the congregation went forward—including Virginia and Renee. Don found great delight in God's overwhelming sense of humor and obvious answer to his prayer.

After the service, Don made his announcement to the church family, "You folks have been so good to us. This is such a wonderful church, and God has blessed our time here. But I know He wants us on the mission field. Within a few weeks, we will be resigning from the church and starting our efforts to raise support." The church family was saddened by the news but absolutely supportive.

Don had never mentioned to Pastor Brown exactly where God had called them, but the next morning Pastor Brown asked, "So when are you going to Japan?" Don saw this as a confirmation that Japan was precisely where God had called him. He was amazed at the many ways God had ordered their steps and prepared them for the future.

Preparing for Japan

Don was once asked whether he believed it was possible to evangelize the world in his generation. The question was a sincere one, posed by

Dr. Chamblers, founder of the World Home Bible League. But as Don pondered his answer, the Lord gently rebuked him. It was not up to Don to determine if it were possible. God said "Go," and it was his responsibility to obey. He would never understand why the Lord chose him, but he was willing and ready to serve.

Although there were many decisions and preparations to be made before the Sisks would actually reach Japan, they began seeking God's immediate direction and following His leading one day and one step at a time.

Following the clear example in Acts 13, Don knew he needed a sending church, and he chose Calvary Baptist Church to be his sending church. He was hesitant, however, to decide on a missions organization. Having recently left the Southern Baptist Convention, he wasn't sure he wanted to be connected again to any organization outside of a local church.

As Don prayed about it, his pastor and several others assured him there were several good missions organizations that did not usurp the authority of local churches. Their primary goal was to support the local church by assisting missionaries in numerous and beneficial ways. The organization was able to legally represent the missionary and take care of many logistical needs. After receiving this counsel, Don's fears were settled, and he began to research which organization he and his family would join. He remembered what he'd learned of Baptist International Missions, Incorporated (BIMI) and the friendship he'd established with its mission board member, Dr. Freeny.

At the time, BIMI was still a young organization and was only supporting a few missionaries, most of which were in Central and South America. But Don noticed the staff had a genuine love for the Lord and His people.

Dr. Freeny took it upon himself to educate Don on all that the mission board represented. Their doctrinal statement, their position on ecclesiastical and personal separation, and their emphasis on soulwinning and church planting on the mission field were just a few of the things that impressed Don. Knowing he shared the same doctrinal beliefs and heart for the lost, Don felt God's peace about BIMI and proceeded to fill out his application.

In June of 1964, Don and Virginia traveled to the BIMI headquarters to meet with the executive board. It had only been a few months since the Sisks has been introduced to independent Baptists, so although they were confident in God's leading, they approached this meeting feeling intimidated. Dr. Lee Roberson, Dr. J.R. Faulkner, Dr. Harold Sightler, Dr. Leroy Perry, Dr. Bill Rice, and Dr. Jack Hudson were just a few of the men present in the meeting. The Sisks gave their résumé and testimonies and answered questions.

After thirty minutes, they were dismissed from the room for a few moments while the board determined their decision. When the Sisks were brought back in, Dr. Freeny announced they had been accepted. Don and Virginia rejoiced as they pillowed their heads that night. They were one step closer to Japan.

Candidate School and Deputation

After acceptance by a mission board, candidate school is typically the next step toward the foreign field. This is a time of training for missionaries before they leave for the field. Don laughs when he recalls how simplistic candidate school was in these early days of BIMI. The totality of their missions training consisted of a few encouraging words such as "God bless you, we'll pray for you, and God will lead." They weren't told what to expect on deputation, how to secure a visa, how to raise support, or how to handle their finances. In fact, they left candidate school with more questions than answers. Yet, they headed back to Illinois trusting the Lord to continue opening doors and giving them the answers they needed.

Deputation began almost immediately. Don remained on staff at Calvary Baptist Church as associate pastor and travelled during his off nights. With a salary of $80 per week, he and his family began scheduling meetings to present their burden for Japan and raise support. They travelled to Illinois, Michigan, and Kentucky for six months and were able to raise $275 per month from the fifteen churches they visited. This money, combined with the support of Calvary Baptist, came to a grand total of $500 per month.

Don had no idea what it would cost to live in Japan. Partially in faith and partially in ignorance, he decided $500 a month would be sufficient for their first term. In reality, this was only 25 percent of what it would cost for a family of four to live in Japan, let alone to take on ministry expenses.

The Sisks' first-term financial provision in Japan was truly a matter of God providing month to month in different and miraculous ways. Don had no idea—then or now—how God made it all happen; he just rejoiced that He did. The most amazing thing about those first few years in Japan was that the providential hand of God and His miraculous provision was more evident than any other time in their lives and ministry since.

The $500 of monthly support seemed so insignificant to the need and to the magnitude of the transition ahead, but God used that support to accomplish many amazing things for His glory. God took what little they had and showed Himself to be more than sufficient.

A missionary once said to Don, "Faith missionaries live from hand to mouth."

Don smiled and thought to himself, "Yes, it's all from God's hand to our mouth." From those early days in Japan they learned to be totally dependent upon God.

Disciple Decisions

With their minimal support raised, the time for the Sisks' departure was drawing close. One of Don's favorite passages of Scripture, Luke 14, came to mind as the family was preparing to leave:

> *If any man come to me, and hate not his father, and mother, and wife, and children, and brethren, and sisters, yea, and his own life also, he cannot be my disciple. And whosoever doth not bear his cross, and come after me, cannot be my disciple...So likewise, whosoever he be of you that forsaketh not all that he hath, he cannot be my disciple.*—LUKE 14:26–27, 33

In this passage the Lord tells His followers what is required to be a disciple: supreme love for Him and total submissiveness to His will. The love the Sisks had for the Lord outweighed their love for their family, possessions, and their home country. But the determining factor in becoming a disciple for the Lord is the capacity to forsake material things in pursuit of the call of Jesus Christ. These discipleship decisions were difficult on a human level, but the Sisks never questioned their call, their love for Christ, or their burden for the people of Japan. They knew the pain of earthly separation and the perception of temporal sacrifice would ultimately pale in comparison to eternity and the inexhaustible love and grace of Jesus.

Little by little, the Lord asked the Sisks to relinquish complete control of their lives to Him. Years earlier, Don had left his steady job in Gary, Indiana, and followed the Lord to Bible college. Several times they had transitioned from stable secular employment or personal investments into positions of lower income with less earning potential. This was a process of learning to allow God to have full reign. With each passing year, the call to Christ became stronger and the allure of the temporal world became weaker.

Each decision point was a test—Jesus over material things, Jesus over temporal things, Jesus over all things. Each decision point was emotional and gut-wrenching. But after each of these difficult decisions of surrender, the Sisks almost immediately experienced the amazing blessing and provision of God in their lives in deeper and more abundant ways than before. They have never regretted even one of these decisions for one moment.

Preparing to Leave for Japan

It was February of 1964, and as the much anticipated and somewhat frightening day of departure to Japan drew closer, God led the Sisks into what felt like even deeper sacrifice. Their faith in the Lord had already been tested in large measure leading up to this day, but now God was requiring them to liquidate their very lives in the States.

Not knowing whether they would ever have these items of convenience again, the Sisk's sold their furniture, washing machine, dryer, carpet, beds, and automobiles. Little by little, their earthly possessions were discharged, and with them, many memories of their first years together as a family.

In it all, God gave more joy than tears. For with the loss of every earthly possession, they were forced to hold more tightly to their Saviour, and they found Him and His will to be more joyful and abundant than their hearts could ever desire.

The Saturday before the Sisks left for Japan, the men of Calvary Baptist Church came together for their weekly 8:00 PM prayer meeting. At the end of the meeting, the men promised Don that every week at the prayer meeting they would be praying for his work in Japan. This promise meant much at the time, but as Don rose to preach several weeks later at 10:00 Sunday morning in Japan, he realized that it was 8:00 PM Saturday night in Illinois, and those prayers meant a great deal more.

It is impossible to describe what the Sisks were feeling emotionally as they arose on what would possibly be their last Sunday in America. Don preached the Sunday morning message. His message was entitled "God will provide—Jehovah-Jireh" from Genesis 22. With many unknowns in his own future, Don preached the message by faith and about faith.

Saying Goodbye

After church that day, the family drove to Chicago's O'Hare Field airport. The drive was quiet as Don and Virginia tried to prepare themselves for the life-changing event that was about to take place. They were going to Japan without so much as a short survey trip. They had never been more than a few hours' drive from where they grew up. Yet now, they courageously left behind the world they knew to embrace a world in need of the Saviour they loved.

When they arrived at the airport, they were overwhelmed by the number of people there to send them off. In addition to Don's parents and two sisters, they saw people representing more than eight different churches—from Harvey to other Chicago-area churches—there to cheer them on their way. This day was a momentous occasion for more reasons than one. Air travel was limited in the mid-1960s, and missionaries were scarce. Now they stood, with the few personal belongings they owned, and faced the reality of the painful goodbye—one unlike anything they had experienced before. This was a goodbye to family, friends, and in essence, everything they knew and loved. It was overwhelmingly emotional, painful, and difficult. Yet, with courage and faith, the Sisks hugged the necks of their family and friends, grasped each other's hands, and the hands of their two children, and together climbed the stairs of an airplane that would take them far from all they had ever known.

Tears flowed. Fear rose. Excitement grew. Anticipation built. This was an experience of emotional extremes—extreme sorrow in the goodbye, extreme anticipation in God's call, extreme courage to get on that plane and follow in obedience.

As the door on the airplane sealed shut, the next chapter in the Sisks life began. Looking at the door, Don thought, "Everyone who loved us is standing right outside of that door." A part of their hearts yearned to walk back off the plane into familiar arms. Yet with resolve, the Sisks said with the Apostle Paul *"For the love of Christ constraineth us"* (2 Corinthians 5:14). They felt like they were leaving familiar arms, but in retrospect, they know they never left the arms of their Saviour. He was with them all the way, and His grace proved sufficient with every step into the unfamiliar.

Don later recalled the strange feeling this complete abandonment brought. He had a sense of awe as he looked out of his window to view America for what he believed was the last time. It felt like closing the casket of a loved one after the last viewing was over. He knew life would never quite be the same.

Nine

THE LORD HUMBLED

1964–1965

There were many stops along the journey to Japan. Their first flight brought them from Chicago to Portland, then Portland to Alaska, and finally from Alaska to Tokyo. This was the Sisks' first experience on a commercial airplane—an experience Don would become more than familiar with over the coming fifty years. The first few bumps of turbulence were unnerving, but as they arrived safely in Japan thousands of miles later, they realized flight bumps were the least of their worries.

The Sisks were physically, emotionally, and mentally exhausted as they stepped onto foreign soil for the first time. With so many new sights, sounds, and smells to take in, the family found themselves overwhelmed—and they immediately realized they would stand out in a crowd. Hundreds of small people were hurrying in every direction. Don, who is 5' 9", remarked of that moment, "The only good feeling upon landing in Japan was that I looked around and noticed I was the tallest person there!"

With eyes wide, the Sisks proceeded through customs and immigration. To their relief, things went smoothly. On the other side of the gate, three missionaries were waiting to greet them—Dave Marcum, Ron White, and George King. Dave had only been in Japan for about six months and Ron for about three weeks. Both men were a tremendous help in the department of empathy. George, a missionary with Baptist Bible Fellowship International, had been in Japan for five years. His knowledge became a great asset to the Sisks as they settled into their work.

A Late Night Walk in Tokyo

Knowing the Sisks would need rest before continuing travel, the three missionaries arranged to stay in Tokyo for the night. Though Don desperately needed rest, he couldn't find it. He awoke around 3:00 AM and began pacing the hotel room. Finally he decided to take a walk and ended up walking the streets of Tokyo alone with God for several hours. As he looked up and down the streets that first night in Japan he thought, "This is home. This is where God has called us. This is the place in which God will allow us to minister." It was surreal.

Don was overcome with gratitude as he realized that after so many years of prayerful preparation and ministry, he was actually walking a Tokyo street. The Lord had directed every step, provided for every need, and been faithful at every uncertainty.

He looked into the night sky and thanked God for choosing him, for calling him to preach, and counting him faithful. He wept with joy at the grace of God. With many unknowns of the future haunting his heart, in that moment he knew and experienced perfect peace. He was certain this was the Lord's doing. He was secure in God's will. He was

CALLED TO PREACH Dr. Don Sisk was born on May 30, 1933, in Nortonville, Kentucky, and he accepted Christ as his Saviour in 1949. He was called to preach on Thanksgiving Day of 1954 at the age of twenty-one. **(Above)** Don Sisk going to the first meeting of Senri Newtown Baptist Church

FAMILY LIFE The Sisks and their two children, Renee and Tim, went on deputation for a year and arrived on the field of Japan in February 1965, as Baptist International Missions, Inc. missionaries. **(Above)** Tim shooting baskets at their home in Akashi **(Top Right)** Don, Virginia, Renee, and Tim **(Bottom Right)** The Sisk family during the early 1970s

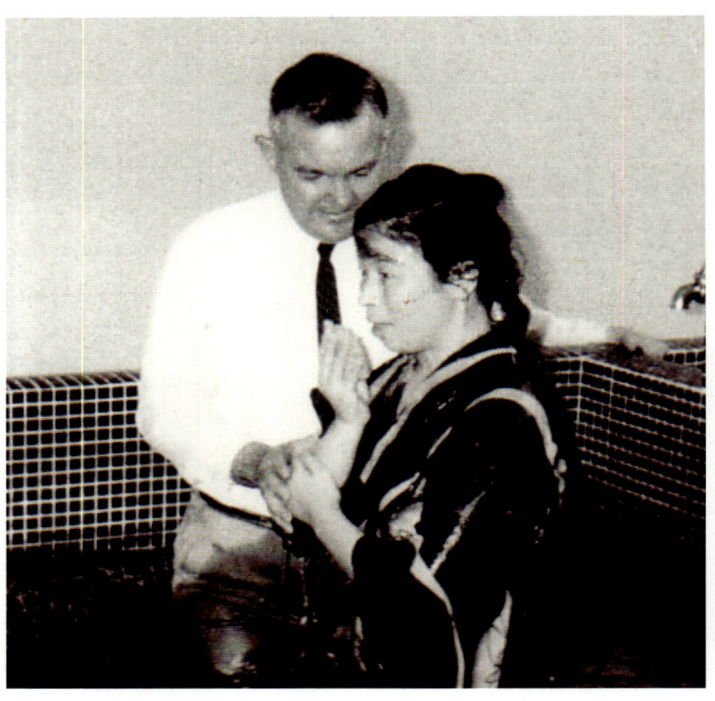

BAPTISMS AND THE CHILDRENS MINISTRY
(Top) Don Sisk baptizing a lady convert at one of Japan's public baths **(Bottom)** "Please get the right shoes"—a common occurrence in the children's ministry

THE OGAWA FAMILY
Sogoro Ogawa was saved at Senri Newtown Baptist Church, Don's first church plant. **(Top)** Ogawa's wedding **(Bottom)** The Ogawas with their children, Luke and Ruth

A CITY CHANGED BY THE GOSPEL **(Above)** An idol burning ceremony at the Senri Newtown Baptist Church **(Top Left)** The youth choir from Kansai Independent Baptist Bible School **(Bottom Left)** Students meeting at Senri Newtown Baptist Church

PROPERTY PURCHASED In October of 1968, the Sisks celebrated the planting of a new church, Grace Baptist Church of Akashi. **(Above)** In 1969, this property was purchased with a $10,000 down payment to be used for Grace Baptist Church and Kansai Independent Baptist Bible School. **(Top Right)** Mrs. Sisk's Sunday School class at Grace Baptist Church in Akashi **(Bottom Right)** Christmas children's meeting with over three hundred children in attendance

第一回卒業式

KANSAI INDEPENDENT BAPTIST BIBLE SCHOOL (Above) This building was constructed within a matter of months, and by 1970 the Kansai Independent Baptist Bible School had a new home. **(Top Left)** First graduation ceremony **(Bottom Left)** First graduating class of six students out of a total student body of thirteen (Dr. Sogoro Ogawa is pictured on the far left.)

UNIQUE OPPORTUNITIES (Above) Don Sisk calling America on a wireless phone at Expo '70 in Japan, which was internationally televised **(Top Right)** Don and Virginia at a Japanese church while Far East Director of Baptist International Missions, Inc. **(Bottom Right)** Virginia receiving a gift from ladies at church in Japan

SENDING FORTH LABORERS In 1973, after planting churches and training national workers in Japan, Dr. and Mrs. Sisk came back to the States, and he served as the Far East Director for BIMI. For ten years, the Sisks traveled around the world, sharing their burden for the needs of Asia. In October 1984, Dr. Sisk became the President and General Director of BIMI. **(Above)** Headquarters for Baptist International Missions, Inc. in Harrison, Tennessee **(Top Right)** Dr. Lee Roberson with Don Sisk at Highland Park Baptist Church **(Bottom Right)** Praying for new BIMI director, Dr. James Ray, in June of 2002

SENRI NEWTOWN BAPTIST CHURCH Since the inception of the church, more than fifty members have given themselves to God for full-time Christian work and have become missionaries or pastors. **(Top)** In 2003, the church dedicated a new 550-seat auditorium. **(Middle Right)** Dr. Sisk with the Ogawas **(Bottom Right)** Senri Newtown Baptist Church auditorium

MENTOR, TEACHER, PREACHER In 2003, Dr. and Mrs. Sisk became members of Lancaster Baptist Church, and Dr. Sisk became the head of the Missions Department at West Coast Baptist College. He and Mrs. Sisk teach in the college and add a wealth of wisdom to the students. **(Above)** Dr. Sisk speaking at a Lancaster Baptist Church couples retreat **(Top Right)** West Coast Baptist College dormitory named Sisk Hall in honor of Don and Virginia Sisk **(Bottom Right)** Dr. Paul Chappell and his wife, Terrie, with Don and Virginia Sisk

IMMEDIATE FAMILY For the last sixty years, Dr. Sisk has given his life to evangelizing. He is a frequent speaker at churches, camps, and conferences around the world. **(Above)** Don and Virginia at Lancaster Baptist Church's 2012 Couples Retreat **(Top Right)** Renee with her husband, Tom, on their fortieth wedding anniversary **(Bottom Right)** Tim with his wife, Donna, on a day off during a missions trip

FAMILY REUNION (Above) Don and Virginia Sisk on their sixtieth wedding anniversary with their children and grandchildren **(Top Left)** Don rejoicing after Kentucky won the national championship in 2012 **(Bottom Left)** The Sisks with their grandchildren and great-grandchildren on Don's eightieth birthday

TODAY (Top) Dr. Don Sisk preaching at Lancaster Baptist Church **(Middle)** Virginia Sisk teaching a ladies class at West Coast Baptist College **(Bottom)** Dr. Sisk teaching future missionaries at West Coast Baptist College

confident that God's hand was with him, in control of those unknowns on the road ahead.

With this perfect peace came wonderful contentment. Don had no physical home and very few physical possessions, but He had a Father who had cared for Him to this very moment in miraculous and wonderful ways. Don poured out his heart to God, thanked Him for His perfect will and peace, and then returned to the hotel where he was able to finally rest for the remainder of the night.

Later that morning the Sisks arose, ate breakfast, and boarded a train from Tokyo to Osaka, where they would be staying with the Marcums. Their new life and work in Japan was just beginning.

Already the Sisks were impressed with their new home. The city was clean, and the people carried themselves with confidence. Sure, it would take time to learn the customs, ways, and language of this people, but they were looking forward to understanding them better in the near future. Most of all, they were eager to introduce them to the love and grace of Jesus Christ.

Cultural Adjustments

Life in Japan moved forward quickly with a variety of new and exciting experiences each day. One day, just after the Sisks arrived in Osaka from Tokyo, they saw a small Toyota station wagon careening down a narrow street at an alarming speed. To make matters worse, the steering wheel was on the wrong side of the car, and the driver was driving on the wrong side of the road. As the car skidded to a stop, none other than Mrs. Marcum hopped out of the car to greet the family. It was moments like these that made Japan seem wonderfully strange…and scary.

Another adjustment was the weather. Although the Sisks were used to cold weather and the temperature in Japan was not as low as in Chicago, it felt much colder because the Japanese people did not use heating systems like Americans. They had small kerosene space heaters that could be moved from room to room depending on which room had the most people. The Marcums owned a large kerosene heater, which they kept in their living room. While the living room was comfortable, the bedrooms were freezing. The result was some sleepless nights while the Sisks learned to adjust.

Overall, the adjustments to Japanese culture ranged from very easy to very difficult, but the Sisks did their best to trust God for His grace day by day. And God was faithful to give the family exactly what they needed exactly when they needed it.

Finding a Place to Live

Dave and Alice Marcum graciously opened their home to the Sisk family until Don was able to find a permanent place to live. Aware of the burden this was surely placing on the Marcums (who had two children of their own), Don immediately began the search for a place his family could call home.

In every place Don visited to inquire about a home, the landlord served him green tea, a symbol of hospitality. The tea reminded Don of weeds, and he found the taste repulsive. Finally, not wanting to be rude, but also reluctant to endure the miserable taste, Don decided to end the suffering quickly by gulping down the whole cup of tea. It didn't take long to discover that this was a really bad idea. Thinking Don enjoyed the tea, the server would quickly refill his cup to the brim. Don realized he should instead sip the tea as slowly and infrequently as possible. To his surprise, over time, he grew to love green tea.

At the third real estate office Don visited, he was able to secure a house that would be theirs for the next three years. The house was situated atop a mountain, a long walk from the train station in Ashiya. Though small, it was nice and in a convenient location. The Sisks managed to make three bedrooms, a kitchen, a living room, and a dining room out of the tight quarters. Just as she always did, Virginia immediately decorated and made the house feel like home.

The exchange rate in Japan at the time of their arrival was 360 yen per dollar, so the $500 of monthly support went much further than it would today. Not only were they able to rent a house, but they were also able to purchase two twin beds. For several weeks, the sum total of their possessions were those two beds, a small electric hot plate, melmac dishes (the popular brand during this time), and a piece of cardboard that served as their dining room table. They pushed the twin beds together, and every night, the entire family would pile into the two beds, happier than they had ever been. Their life during those few weeks was a testimony to the truth that joy is not a product of material possessions; joy is a product of obeying God in faith.

Transition and Trials

The new life was not without hardships. Every day brought new fears and doubts. At times, it seemed the fears and doubts were more prevalent than faith and courage. Every day they woke up feeling displaced and disoriented, wondering how they would ever minister to the people of Japan. It was hard enough to acclimate to a new culture and new relationships, much less to strategize effective gospel ministry in this new place.

During these days they learned more fully what it meant to trust God one day at a time. As a family, they claimed Matthew 6:34, *"Take therefore no thought for the morrow: for the morrow shall take thought for the things of itself. Sufficient unto the day is the evil thereof."* "One day at a time" became a spiritual focus in their transition, for each day was overwhelming. With the daily plethora of unanswered questions and fears, they could rely only on the Lord to meet their needs for that day alone. He had called them to Japan and they believed He would provide for them and use them to accomplish His will.

God used the Marcums greatly in Don's life. The dedication of this family was astounding. They had only been on the field for seven months but had studied the language diligently and were already conversing well. Even the Japanese people would comment that the Marcums "are very gifted in the language."

It didn't take Don long, however, to realize that the Marcums' mastery of Japanese was more than "a gift." Late one night while the Sisks were still living with the Marcums, Don went into the kitchen to get a drink for Tim. He was surprised to find the kitchen light on and Dave Marcum sitting at the kitchen table diligently studying Japanese. It was at that moment that Don realized if he wanted to learn Japanese, it was going to take dedication and many, many hours of study. It was "a gift" that could only come through sacrifice and hard work.

Don and Virginia began language school a week after arriving in Japan. Their classes took place in Kobe, just nine miles from Ashiya. Hopeful of cultural acquisition, they decided to take the train, which only cost a few cents and would afford the opportunity to learn the train system. Actually getting on the train, however, proved to be more difficult than they had imagined. Without knowing the language, they couldn't read the signs and had no idea which train to catch. One cold morning in particular froze itself into their memory as they stood watching trains fly past them—humiliated. In frustration, Don told Virginia, "This is stupid. We have studied more than sixteen years each, but we don't even know enough to read and catch a train!"

As they began their first language class, the feeling of humiliation returned. They sat before a teacher at a small table in a cold room heated only by a small space heater (which was turned off the majority of the time). Don knew the lessons were necessary, but he still felt silly as the teacher said things like: "This is a pencil. This is a desk. This is a book."

After pastoring for several years, teaching in a Bible college, and preaching in revivals and Bible conferences, it felt degrading to be required to sit and relearn the basics of language. Yet this was where God had them at this moment, and they had no choice but to walk through the valleys He ordained. The Lord used humbling moments like these to bring the Sisks to greater dependence upon His grace.

Hearing from Home

Communication with friends and family in America was practically nonexistent during their first term in Japan. Overseas phone calls at the time cost $25 for just three minutes, and the Sisks had no discretionary income for costly phone calls. In fact, during their first three years in Japan, they received only two phone calls from the States.

Every month a few letters would come in the mail, which always brought excitement to their hearts. Occasionally, a care package would arrive from Don's mother. These boxes would consist of items they could not get in Japan—peanut butter, Tootsie Rolls, pinto beans, and other supplies the family enjoyed. These care packages became more than physical pleasures; they were sources of grace, love, and encouragement from home. Their arrival became one of the highlights of each month.

One day, a box sent by a stateside church arrived during a language lesson. Unable to contain their excitement, Don and Virginia opened it immediately. Their hearts sank when they discovered the box was filled with unpractical items, primarily old and outdated clothing that didn't fit anyone in the family. One particular dress looked like it was from the Roaring Twenties. Don teased Virginia that they should take a picture of her in the dress to send back to the church that sent the box. In the end, the contents of that "care package" supplied the family with cleaning rags. Although certainly well meaning, it was obvious that the people who sent the box had not considered the Sisks' actual needs. This memory has served Don well, and he today encourages well-meaning Christians to be thoughtful in how they express their love and care to missionaries.

Renee and Tim Adjust to Their New Lives

Renee was twelve and Tim four when the Sisks moved to Japan, and there was a long period of adjustment with plenty of unique struggles for both of the children.

Renee missed her school and friends back in the States and found it difficult to find a place for herself in her new home. In Japan, she attended a school called Canadian Academy, which had been started to serve the international community in the Kobe area. There were several nationalities attending the school, which made for a multicultural environment. (Parent-teacher meetings at the school were interesting because of the language barriers. While the meeting was conducted primarily in English, afterward Don could hear over fifteen languages being spoken by the people in the room.)

Academically, the school was advanced—significantly more so than the public schools Renee had attended in Illinois. The first few months in Japan were devoted to helping her catch up to the other students in her grade. Renee never complained as she tackled her studies, and she worked diligently to learn a new language and culture. Overall, she navigated a difficult transition at a critical time in her life with grace and faith.

Because Tim was only four, the Sisks decided to do as other missionaries had done and put him in a Japanese kindergarten to accelerate his learning of Japanese. While this worked for some children, it didn't work for Tim. One morning, just a few weeks after Tim had started school, Don went to the post office in Ashiya. Out of the corner of his eye he saw a little boy walking alone down the street. Thinking this was odd, Don turned to find that it was his own son. Tim's teachers had let him out of class by himself although he was only four years old.

In shock, Don ran to pick up his son, headed right back to the school, and politely informed the administrator and teacher that Tim would no longer be attending. This was exciting news to Tim's little ears; he never liked that school in the first place.

After the kindergarten situation was resolved, Tim's adjustment to Japan was exceptional. In fact, by the time he was in first grade, he was commuting to school by train with his sister. As his classes finished an hour and a half earlier than hers, he took the train home alone. Within months, Tim was as good as any Japanese citizen at train travel through Japan, and he quickly became fluent in Japanese.

Meanwhile, Don and Virginia were still busy with language school. One day their Japanese teacher told them she would be happy to give them lessons in their own home if it would be more convenient. The teacher lived close, so it was a welcome change to purchase her train pass rather than their own and pick her up at the station. This worked out wonderfully for the whole family. Not only was their home warmer than the school, but now Tim could nap comfortably at home during his parents' lessons. They studied every day from 1:00–3:00 in the afternoon. Learning Japanese required a huge amount of concentration and outside work, but Don and Virginia were committed to the task.

Learning to Worship in a New Language

Sundays were the hardest for the Sisks. Since arriving in Japan they had not attended an English service. The Marcums and Whites were planting the Kita Guchi Baptist Church and had rented a Japanese kindergarten room for services on Sundays and Wednesdays. All services were conducted through an interpreter; even the singing and announcements were in Japanese. When Don arrived, the three missionaries began to rotate the preaching. Just a few weeks after the Sisk's arrival, however, Dave Marcum began preaching in Japanese on his turns.

Don and Virginia missed their home church and missed hearing English singing and preaching. Although they soon learned enough Japanese writing to be able to read and sing hymns with the Japanese Christians, they had no idea what they were singing.

At Calvary Baptist Church in Illinois, the Sisks had been accustomed to an aggressive soulwinning ministry. The church averaged four hundred in Sunday attendance and saw people come to Christ nearly every week. Don was used to teaching Sunday school and preaching on a regular basis while also heading up the visitation program.

The contrast from America to Japan was difficult. The Sisks suddenly found themselves attending a small service with about fifteen people on a good day. Don had little to no responsibility, and they were unable to go soulwinning until they learned the language. All of this, along with a different atmosphere and spirit during the services, made the Sisks feel helpless, far from home, and as if their whole ministry world had come to a grinding halt. For a time, the couple struggled to be excited about Sunday services.

Because the services were so vastly different in Japan, the Sisks treasured any English-speaking service that was sent to them. Occasionally, their home church would send a recording of a church service. At these times, the family would gather and have their own special service. Don and Virginia did their best to instill the Word of God into their children at home. They often had devotions together as a family, and sometimes Don would teach Renee and Tim a Sunday school lesson. On Sundays, the missionary wives would teach the younger children a class in English while the Japanese service was in progress.

The three missionaries shared the expense of renting the building, buying gospel tracts, paying utilities, and covering other ministry expenses. Since all three were relatively new to Japan, it was a good cooperative relationship and experience for them. In hindsight, having more English-speaking people (with three missionary families) than

Japanese probably discouraged the Japanese from feeling ownership of the church. But since there were no other BIMI missionaries in the country and all three families were relatively new to missions work, it was all they knew to do at the time. In spite of the less than ideal situation, God blessed their labor together.

Every Friday evening, the three missionary families would meet for a time of fellowship, tract preparation, and prayer, rotating homes and meal preparation. They enjoyed refreshments such as coffee and cake or pie. The fellowship was uplifting and needed, especially as these couples were spending an average of six hours each day studying Japanese. Friday evenings became a welcomed break when they could relax and bear one another's burdens.

The First Fruits of Faith

Early each Saturday morning, the three men would travel by train to Nishinomiya, where the kindergarten classroom for Sunday services was located. They would spend the entire day passing out thousands of Japanese tracts. Most Saturdays, there was no visible fruit from their labor, but often, God would use those tracts to bring Japanese guests to church the next day.

One Sunday, Iwata—a distinguished-looking man in his mid-thirties—came to church after receiving an invitation the day before. That night, Don preached from Ephesians 2:8–10 with the help of an interpreter. At the end of the service, Iwata came forward with pleading eyes and asked how he could know Jesus personally. With the aid of an interpreter, Don led his first Japanese soul to Jesus Christ. After trusting Christ, Iwata told Don his story.

His wife had recently committed suicide. Filled with great sorrow and despair, he, too, had been contemplating suicide. But when he received the pamphlet the day before, he thought, "Maybe this can help me." The next day he decided to go to church, and he found the help he was looking for in Jesus Christ. That Sunday night was a glorious night for the three missionary families. They were grateful to see God work and begin to reward their labor of faith and love.

Iwata wonderfully grew in his new faith. Just a few weeks later he was baptized and began attending the weekly church services. He soon became a willing and joyful volunteer at the church, and over time he became a wonderful blessing and friend to the missionaries.

A Dark Challenge

Before leaving for Japan, Don anticipated challenges related to language and culture adjustment, although not fully aware just how difficult they would be. But in the spring of 1965, Don faced a challenge he never expected—depression.

The depression didn't come overnight; it crept in slowly—little by little, day by day, disappointment by disappointment, until Don found himself enveloped in a dark cloud. He had never envisioned having to battle such emotional lows. In his heart, God's call was a blessed, joyful, delightful opportunity. But that spring and summer brought a season of despair that Don never forgot.

It started as the stifling heat of summer descended. The Sisks' monthly support was low, so they had no air conditioning. Japanese summers are extremely hot and humid, and without even a fan for circulation, the heat was almost unbearable. The Japanese people were suffering as well, for, rather than carry handkerchiefs, they literally carried towels to soak up the sweat resulting from the oppressive heat. The Sisks began to do the same.

To make matters worse, their Japanese teacher informed them she would be taking a six-week break. They tried to explain to her their concern about taking a break from language school. They were progressing well, had no money for vacation themselves, and desperately needed to continue learning the language as quickly as possible. However, she explained that every teacher in Japan takes a six-week vacation. She gave them no other option but to wait for her return.

With millions of lost people surrounding him, Don found himself silenced. He had the truth and was desperate to tell others, but he had no ability to do so. He did what little he could, but it truly felt pointless. He passed out gospel tracts and invited the people to read them, but as soon as they began asking questions, Don could not help them. With his language teacher away for six weeks, he was losing hope of being able to communicate with them. This left Don feeling useless, and he felt more so with every passing day.

That summer Don lost the joy that had been his since the day he accepted Christ. In reality, he was exactly where God had placed him, trying to do what God called him to do. But without a handle on the language, he felt handicapped, utterly frustrated, and discouraged. He didn't have the emotional energy to respond spiritually, and he wasn't sure what to do next.

In this dark season, God directed Don to a book on his shelf he had never read. Years earlier, he had heard John Edmond Haggai preach at a convention in Kentucky and had purchased his book, *How to Win over Worry*. Don pulled the book from his shelf and began reading.

The book's premise was based on Philippians 4:4–9, which begins *"Rejoice in the Lord alway...."* The author began by admonishing Christians to always rejoice. He explained that Christians should never worry about anything. Don was immediately convicted. The author continued to explain that God was interested in every detail of His children's lives, so they should not only give all their problems to God, but also always give thanks for every problem.

Now Don was becoming frustrated. In fact, the further he read the more frustrated he became. He even became angry. He thought to himself, "If I were living in Kentucky where Haggai lives and I had a big salary like he does and was a popular speaker like he is and didn't have to learn Japanese, I could write a book like this, too. He has no idea what people like me are experiencing!"

Don's pity party continued until he came to a chapter where the author gave a personal illustration. The physician who had delivered Haggai's son had been drinking and put too much pressure on the baby's head, causing brain damage. At the time the book was written his son was a teenager but still suffered from severe brain damage. In fact, the boy could do nothing for himself. His parents were required to be full-time caregivers for him. Suddenly, Don's thinking changed as God's truth broke through to him.

This author really did know what he was talking about. But even if he didn't, the human author of Philippians certainly did. Paul penned the words *"Rejoice in the Lord alway,"* not from a luxurious resort, but from a prison cell. The Holy Spirit inspired him to tell people of all ages to rejoice in the Lord no matter their circumstances.

Through Haggai's personal testimony and the truth of Philippians 4:4, Don saw his discouragement for the self-pity it was. He repented of his sin and apologized to Virginia, Renee, and Tim for not being a spiritual leader as a husband and father through this time.

Don determined that day that if he never learned Japanese or won another soul to the Lord, and that if he never started a church or did the things the Lord laid on his heart, he would nonetheless rejoice in the Lord. From that day forward, Don made it a practice to remind himself every day to rejoice in the Lord. If he could not rejoice in the circumstances, he could always rejoice in the Lord.

A Tempting Opportunity

In the midst of Don's battle with depression, the Sisks faced one of the most trying situations of their first term. It came as a result of one the very few phone calls they received from the States. Don was awakened one night by a call from his pastor in Harvey, Illinois, who told Don the church had tried to find a replacement for him but was unable to, so the deacons wanted to offer Don his old position as associate pastor, with a sizeable raise. They even offered to pay all the Sisks' expenses for moving back to America.

The timing of this call was remarkable. With the many difficulties they'd recently experienced, Don's flesh immediately wanted to cry out, "Yes! We'll be there in a few days!" Everything within him wanted to jump at the opportunity to return to the familiar family and friends in Illinois. Instead, Don expressed his shock that the conversation had taken place and told Pastor Brown that while he didn't believe returning would be God's will for his life, he would pray about the matter out of respect for their friendship.

Don returned to bed with a heavy heart to find Virginia awake and curious as to what had happened. When Don told her about the phone call, she began to weep. Their hearts craved escape from this unfamiliar and difficult place, and they wondered why the Lord would allow them to be taunted by this opportunity. Feeling overwhelmed and alone, they prayed together.

It's difficult to put words to what God does in our hearts when we pray. That night, God reassured Don and Virginia that He was with them, they were in the center of His will, and He would give them the grace to go forward. Don wrote a letter to the church the next day explaining that although he loved and respected them, he could not leave the place where God had called him to serve. This would not be the last temptation the Sisks would face, but with God's grace they stayed the course and continued to obey God at every decision point.

Finally, a Chance to Preach in Japanese

The summer passed, and with it, the heat and Don's depression. Language school resumed, and Don was thankful for God's grace and glad that he hadn't made a bad decision during a discouraging season.

By November of 1965, Don was preparing his first message in Japanese. He started by writing the message in English, then with the help of his teacher, translating it into Japanese. He practiced preaching the message for three weeks. After it was fully translated, he read it repeatedly. He read it to Virginia. He read it to the children. He walked to the mountains to pray and read it again. And again. In time, he felt confident he could communicate the message effectively by reading it to the congregation.

The night to preach finally arrived. The Kita Guchi Baptist Church congregation was still small; that Sunday evening, there were eight or ten Japanese people in attendance. The room was stuffy due to the small space heater. Don stood and began to read the sermon, and almost instantly became frustrated. He kept losing his place in the notes and had difficulty finding it again. After thirty minutes, he was finished. It was the most embarrassing, if not the most miserable, thirty minutes of his entire life.

If there were any doubt whether or not the message was a failure, one of the Japanese Christians prayed this sincere but crushing prayer at the end of the service: "Dear Lord, thank you for Don Sisk. We love him, but please help him. We didn't understand what he was saying." When Don walked through the door of his home that night he was crushed. He prayed with his family and then wept most of the night. He told the Lord that it had not been his idea to come to Japan. He knew God had led him there, yet he felt completely inadequate and questioned if he would ever be able to preach in Japanese.

Hindsight is always clearer, and Don realized later that it had been a mistake to attempt to preach in Japanese after studying the language for only eight months. But he didn't realize that was the problem then. He simply had to let go of his disappointment and press forward.

A Miraculous Answer to Prayer

Every Friday at 6:00 AM the three missionaries met together for a one-hour prayer meeting. The Friday following Don's attempt to preach in Japanese, he asked the men to pray that God would give him a proficient, Bible-believing, Baptist interpreter. He had prayed over the matter, and he believed God wanted him to start a church with the help of an interpreter. The other two men thought he was joking. They told him, "Don, there isn't an interpreter like that in Japan." And as far as Don knew, there wasn't. But that was why he needed them to pray.

It was at a Christmas party just a few days later (December, 1965) that God amazingly answered this prayer of faith. There at this party, Don met Keita Takagi. Keita had studied in America for four years, where he had heard the gospel, trusted Christ, and grown into an energetic soulwinner. He had just recently returned to Japan for one year before heading back to America to attend seminary. To top it off, his English was flawless.

From the moment they met, it seemed that Keita Takagi and Don shared a God-given chemistry. They found themselves in the corner discussing what each of them was planning and praying for God to do. Keita said, "Don, I am praying about working with some missionaries for a few months. I am going back to seminary in August of next year. But for the next few months I would like to work with a missionary in starting a new church."

Don could not believe God was answering his prayer so quickly and so profoundly. He stood there staring at the man in amazement. He felt like one of the believers in Acts 12 who had prayed for Peter to be released from prison but then could not believe that God had actually answered their prayer.

Don invited Keita to their home to further discuss working together. Virginia made delicious Kentucky fried chicken for the men, which Don later discovered was Keita's favorite meal. (Don suggests that it was the fried chicken that ultimately enticed Keita to work with the family in planting a church.)

Those first months in Japan involved some of the most humbling and stretching experiences of Don's life. He had very little to provide for his family and no means to work for more. He was reduced to communication on a toddler's level. He battled a grueling season of discouragement. He felt limited and hampered in ministry on every side. Simply put, missionary work was not what he had anticipated or expected.

Yet, God used these very hardships to prepare Don for a work that was greater than he ever dreamed possible. The season of humbling was not a waste. Rather, it was preparation for an outpouring of blessing that was coming just around the next bend in the road.

Ten
THE LORD RENEWED

1965–1966

Meeting Keita Takagi was as providential an event as Don had ever experienced in his life. Their meeting over fried chicken had proven to be God's direct answer to prayer on many levels. Having come through a dark season of discouragement, Don and Virginia were in need of renewal from God. They longed to see His intervention in ways that would remind them of His presence and promise. Keita was the first of many providential interventions soon to come.

Welcome to Senri Newtown

Keita agreed to work with the Sisks and had great ideas on how to get started. He told Don of a place near his home city of Senriyama, a new town named Senri Newtown made up primarily of high-rise apartment buildings. Only a few months prior, this new town had been vacant, but over the previous months, more than eighty thousand people had moved into the area. Before Keita left that night, they agreed to meet at Senri Newtown and survey the city.

The next Friday morning, as Don stepped off of the train in Senri Newtown for the first time, he was overcome by the span of high-rise apartments and the sheer number of people rushing in every direction. God began to burden his heart that there was not a gospel witness in this highly populated new city. It was immediately obvious to Don that this was the place God wanted him to plant a church and minister with the gospel. His mind filled with questions and ideas: Where would they meet? When could they begin? It was as if God reignited his original vision, and Don's heart revived with hope and anticipation of what God would do in this place.

Later that day, after Don and Keita toured the city and spent time in prayer together, they visited the office in charge of renting space for public meetings. Keita was certain they would not rent out a building for religious purposes, but Don explained to the person in charge that they would also be teaching English and working to assist the developing community. From that point forward in the discussion, the man in charge became welcoming. He agreed to rent one of the rooms in the main building.

The room they were able to rent was not only convenient, but it was incredibly accessible to the public. The building was only a few feet from the train station and was known by most people in town. It was a miracle from God that they were able to rent a room at all; that He would give them this room that exceeded all expectations was doubly miraculous. The rent for the room was reasonable, $25 for a day, so they decided to begin using it on Sunday mornings and evenings. On Wednesdays they planned to meet in a smaller room to save money.

Senri Newtown Baptist Church

With a translator to partner with and plans for a new church underway, Don felt like he had been set free! Finally, he could communicate the gospel with the people he was called to reach.

Within days, Don and Keita had chosen a launch date and began to spread the news through word of mouth and the local newspaper about the Senri Newtown Baptist Church. They also printed twenty thousand pamphlets to deliver from apartment to apartment. For weeks, the men did everything they knew to do: door-to-door visitation, passing out pamphlets in front of the train station, and going all over the city with a loudspeaker announcing the meeting.

Although things were beginning to fall into place, Don knew that without prayer, they would quickly unravel. He rented a room in a nearby park specifically for the purpose of prayer, and he and Keita set aside the Monday and Tuesday prior to the first service to do nothing but fast, pray, and seek God's power for the services.

Several missionaries joined in the effort and assisted in the preparation for the first meeting of Senri Newtown Baptist Church. Missionary Robin McElroy, who was serving in Tokyo, came to lead the singing for the service. Missionary Ron White played the piano, and Renee Sisk played the organ. Ron White, Dave Marcum, and others from the church in Nishinomiya came to help distribute pamphlets, as well as helping in many other areas. God assembled a great team of people to prepare for that first Sunday.

From experience, Don knew that ministry was never a one-man show. As the first service of the new church approached, Don was overwhelmed by the many people, all over the world, who had a part in it. Literally hundreds of people were praying, giving, and training for he and his family to get to the mission field, stay there, and do the work God had called them to do. Don felt a deep gratitude for those who were helping him in the work in Japan, as well as those who were making his ministry possible from the states. He marveled that people would give toward the salvation of souls whom they would never meet this side of Heaven. With these gifts came a great sense of responsibility and accountability. He truly wanted to see fruit abound to their account.

With hundreds of hours of work and prayer poured out and many years of preparation invested, the evening of the first service came with overwhelming anticipation. The night before, Don's excitement was nearly unbearable—he lay wide awake most of the night, dreaming of what God would do. What happened when the doors opened the next evening at 6:30 PM was phenomenal.

The First Service in Senri Newtown

The first service was held in February of 1966. The invitations had been printed in the form of a ticket. As people arrived that night, they presented their tickets at the entrance. Of course, everyone was welcome whether or not they had a ticket, but the tickets seemed to create an incentive for people to attend and even to be early.

Christian workers were standing outside the building directing people into the room and giving out information pamphlets to those passing by. Every few minutes, with heart racing, Don bolted up the stairs to the meeting room and watched with amazement as the room began to fill up.

One young man, a graduate student in English at nearby Kansai University, approached Don and boldly stated he had no interest in Christianity. Since Don was going to preach in English with an interpreter, he was simply interested in practicing his language skills.

At first Don was disappointed. *I didn't come seven thousand miles so someone could practice English.* Then he laughed, because his "Kentuckian" English was not likely to be a great asset to anyone studying English anyway. He decided to rejoice at every soul who walked through the doors no matter their reason for being there. And he began to pray that God would turn their hearts to Jesus.

By 7:00 the room was filled with approximately sixty people, the majority of whom had never once stepped into a Christian service before. Workers gave each person two gifts for visiting: a small New Testament and a hymnal with about twenty hymns. After a beautiful song service, Don preached from Paul's message at Mars Hill. He spoke about the unknown God and introduced a roomful of lost Japanese hearts to the Lord Jesus Christ.

The First Souls Saved at Senri Newtown

After the gospel message, Don extended an invitation, asking if anyone would like to know Jesus Christ as their Lord and Saviour. Eleven people lifted their hands that night, among them the graduate student—Sogoro Ogawa—who had claimed complete disinterest in Christianity. Sogoro was a reminder to Don that the truth of the gospel can penetrate even the hardest hearts. He was glad he had chosen to welcome the young man into the service that night instead of focusing on his reason for coming.

Just a few weeks later, Sogoro was the first person Don was privileged to baptize in Japan. From the day of his salvation, Sogoro showed great signs of leadership. He grew quickly in God's grace and developed a tremendous heart for God. He was a diligent student of the Bible and energetically told others about the gospel. Don mentored Sogoro in the same way that Paul trained Timothy, spending more time with Sogoro than anyone other than his own family. This investment would prove very fruitful in years to come.

Of the eleven who were saved that first night, seven were baptized and became faithful members of the church over the ensuing months.

Services at Senri Newtown continued to be well-attended. On their first Sunday morning service there were fifty people present. The average attendance in an established church in Japan at the time was only twenty-five people. Don was in awe that God brought so many people to Senri Newtown so quickly.

Discipling Believers and Developing the Church

From the very beginning, discipleship was a foundational value of the Senri Newtown Baptist Church. Keita quickly put together discipleship lessons that were distributed in the following weeks to each person who made a profession of faith.

With each passing week, God gave Don and those working with him wonderful visits with new Japanese people. He was moving in hearts, and before long the church outgrew the small building they rented for their Wednesday services. The new Christians were hungry for God's Word and for Christian fellowship, so they quickly became faithful to all three services during the week. It was amazing to see God develop their hearts for His Word and His people.

It typically takes a significant period of time for a new church plant in a foreign country to become indigenous (self-supporting and self-sustaining). In the beginning, the missionaries do most of the work, supply much of the funds, and do nearly all of the preaching, praying, singing, and discipling of young converts. Don spent much time investing into the members knowing that one day the responsibilities of the church would transfer to them.

Every Sunday, the Sisks rose early to make the ninety-minute drive from Ashiya to Senri Newtown. With the help of other believers, they prepared the room for services by cleaning, setting up chairs, bringing in the pulpit and organ, and distributing the hymnals and New Testaments. The room the group rented was typically used for parties on Saturdays, so when the Sisks came in to set up on Sunday, they were often picking up beer cans and other trash from the night before. (As Sunday is a holiday for Japanese workers, the building's custodial crew had the day off.) It was an inconvenience, but the Sisks were grateful to have a room and were more than willing to do whatever it took to keep it in good condition for their growing church family.

Because of the distance from their house to the church, the Sisks would spend Sunday afternoons in Senri Newtown. They rented a little office for these occasions. Many times their Sunday noon meal would consist only of a bowl of curry rice, which they grew to love. Tim's favorite meal on Sundays was an egg salad sandwich followed by cake, which every young boy in Japan loved.

Sunday afternoons were a great time for the Sisk family to reconnect, but they were also a time of prayer and fellowship with the members of the church. Don and the other men often conducted street meetings, and they were always busy inviting new people to the services. Then on Sunday evenings, many of the members would stay after service for fellowship.

Though weary by the end of the day, Don and his family relished this time after service. They understood that outside of the church, these new believers had little to no fellowship with other Christians. Even though it meant arriving home late and heading to school exhausted the next morning, the Sisks tried their best to provide as much fellowship as possible. Sunday was a time for new Christians to be recharged for the Lord, and the Sisks did everything they could to help them grow.

Miracles are Worth the Wait

With the launch of Senri Newtown Baptist Church, God began to move in a remarkable way. Many young people accepted Christ and developed hearts for God in the early days of the church. A fervency quickly grew in their hearts to spread the gospel in the country of Japan. In time, God would use many of them in full-time ministry.

Don came to look back on those beginning days with great delight. It seemed there were so many difficulties preceding these blessings, but seeing God work in Japanese hearts made the waiting, the discouragement, the financial sacrifices, and the burdens all worth it. When those first souls came to Christ that Sunday evening, Don knew that all of the trials and transitions had been for that very purpose. As he met these precious hearts, he felt as if he knew them already, for he had dreamed of them, prayed for them, wept for them, and loved them long before he ever met them. His heart soared to finally see God at work, fulfilling the call he had initiated so many years before.

Patience played a major role in seeing the blessings of God at Senri Newtown. So often Don had been tempted to quit or turn back. So many times he had doubted and questioned what God was doing and why. God's timetable didn't make sense. But as the waiting gave way to harvesting, he was glad that God had given him the grace to endure.

In reality, what God did at Senri Newtown was miraculous. That just one year after the Sisks arrived in Japan they would be planting a church was amazing. That it would see such immediate fruit was unheard of. This was undoubtedly the Lord's doing, and the Sisks rejoiced to be involved.

Eleven

THE LORD STRETCHED

1966

The Saturday before the first service at Senri Newtown, Don mentally reviewed all he needed to do before the service. It was then that the Lord reminded him he had not paid the rent for the building. The payment was only $200, but Don had spent everything they had in preparation for their first service. He was three days late and out of physical resources, but he knew there was one resource that would never run out: prayer. So Don began to pray that God in His own way would provide the money for the rent.

On Monday and Tuesday of the next week, he went to the post office hoping there would be money in the mail. Nothing.

On Wednesday he went again, still praying. Almost nothing—just two pieces of mail. One was a letter from a church stating how excited they were to hear about the first service at Senri Newtown, and the other was a letter from a friend and soulwinning partner in Kentucky named Jimmy Hughes. Jimmy was a kind man, but Don knew he couldn't expect any money from him. In fact, Don would have liked to send *him* money. A disabled veteran living off of a meager veteran's pension, Jimmy was barely making ends meet.

Disappointed with no letters promising funds, Don trudged home to his office where he opened the letter from Jimmy. They had not stayed in touch for years, so Don looked forward to hearing news from his old friend. To his surprise, this letter contained not one, but two checks inside for $100 each. The first check was dated January 15, 1966, and the second was dated the day after. There was no way, other than the Lord, that Jimmy could have known that Don needed exactly $200.

The Lord certainly works in mysterious ways. Don knew hundreds of people who had an abundance of resources, and any one of them could have given Don the money without feeling its loss. Yet, God had chosen to use Jimmy, a man with practically nothing, to answer Don's prayer. God spoke to Don's heart that day, reminding him that how He chose to answer prayers was none of Don's business. Sitting at his desk with those two checks in his hand, Don smiled with delight at God's faithfulness and power.

A Growing Church of New Believers

Senri Newtown Baptist Church had few programs in its beginning days. Discipleship was the primary focus, and Don and Keita delivered the lessons directly to the homes of the new believers, which proved to be a great source of growth. Although Don was unable to spend a lot of one-on-one time working through the lessons, the new Christians always had their lessons completed on time. The program was a great source of growth for the new church family.

ELEVEN—THE LORD STRETCHED

For the first several months of church life, there was no program specifically for children. Because of the receptiveness of children, Don wanted to have children's meetings from the start. However, Keita advised differently. With insight into his own culture, he told Don that most Japanese men believe church is primarily for women and children, thus it may be best to wait a few months. Don didn't want to agree, but after prayer, he recognized that Keita knew far more about the culture and people of Japan, so he would be wise to heed this advice.

After the church was four months old, they decided to begin hosting children's meetings in various places around the area. Since neither Virginia nor Don were able to give the lessons in Japanese, they solicited the help of the new believers, which proved to aid in developing the Bible knowledge and ministry experience of young Christians. Virginia would prepare the lesson and then teach it to the other teachers using a combination of Japanese and English resources. As a result of their preparation together, the new Christians grew rapidly. And over the years, the children's meetings also grew immensely. By the time Don and Virginia completed their ministry in Senri Newtown, over four hundred children were in attendance every Sunday morning.

Originally, the children's meeting was held early on Sunday morning, and then the adults would come back to the meeting place for the Sunday morning service. Additional rooms were rented for Monday and Tuesday services held as additional outreach. The goal of the weekday meetings was to have the people in attendance begin coming on Sundays.

Several other outreaches also continued to flourish as the church began to grow. Park meetings, street meetings, tract distribution, and door-to-door visitation would almost always end in a prayer meeting in a little office the Sisks rented. The room was only 6'x9' and was often filled with more than thirty people gathering to pray. Looking back, Don can not fathom how all of this was accomplished for the Lord. It was God and God alone.

Baptisms Every Month

From the very beginning of Senri Newtown Baptist Church, it was a rare occasion when there wasn't at least one soul saved on a Sunday. Because of the numbers of those being saved, the church planned a baptismal service once a month. Many times in Japan, a church would go an entire *year* without one baptism. But the first year alone, Don was privileged to baptize *eighty-nine* Japanese Christians. The number of people being saved and baptized at Senri Newtown Baptist Church was truly a marvelous blessing and moving of God.

At the time, very few Japanese had baths in their homes; instead, they were accustomed to bathing in *ofuroba*, or public baths. As these normally did not open until 4:00 PM, Don arranged with the owners of a local *ofuroba* to use the facility right after the morning service for baptism. Often the owners, present during the baptisms, would stand to the side and watch in wonder as people stepped forward to be immersed under the water. At each baptism service, Don explained the gospel and the significance of baptism.

The Japanese word for "Baptist" is *Baputesuto*—a word which most Japanese people had never heard and did not understand what it meant. Some Americans thought it would be better not to use the word at all, since the Japanese didn't understand its meaning anyway. Don, however, after giving the matter much thought and prayer, came to the conclusion that the word was biblical and should remain in the church name.

The Yamashiro Family

The wonderful stories of God's work at Senri Newtown are manifold—too many for one book. As the Sisks faithfully went door-to-door with the gospel and visited with new believers, God continued to work in this new church. Visits with new believers, in particular, often presented the opportunity to meet and minister to other family members or friends.

One especially memorable family was that of a young lady named Sachiko Yamashiro, who was saved in the first meeting at Senri Newtown. Sachiko's father was not saved; in fact, he was a priest of Tenrikyo Shintoism. He was a middle-aged man who had a strong dislike for both Americans and Christians as his particular form of Shintoism was opposed to both.

Don tried to speak with him at every opportunity, even if it meant trying to stand in the doorway to get his attention. Over a period of time, he gradually began to warm up to Don, and once he allowed Don to bring a recorded message by a Japanese evangelist. Sitting with his wife and daughter, Mr. Yamashiro pretended to be disinterested, but it was obvious to Don that the Lord was speaking to him through the recorded message.

A few days later, Mr. Yamashiro and his wife visited the church for the first time. They listened, but did not respond. Don was thrilled when they returned for the next three weeks, each time listening with greater interest. The Sisks continued to pray, and after a month of visiting church, the Yamashiros came forward one Sunday during the invitation and said, "We have decided to take Jesus as our Saviour." One of the church members took a Bible and showed them how they could be saved. Both trusted Christ that day and grew to be two of the most dedicated believers Don has ever seen.

Shortly after his conversion, Mr. Yamashiro invited Don to his house and showed him a room lined with shelves and shelves of idols and asked Don to help him dismantle the room. Don was only too happy to do so, and together, with a hammer and crowbar, the men took down the shelves and put the idols in a box.

Mr. Yamashiro handed Don the box and said, "Teacher, I don't have any more need for my idols. Do with them whatever you would like." Don put the box in his station wagon along with the crowbar and hammer and broke them up at his house. He brought the pieces to church the next Sunday evening and after the service piled the pieces together in an open field and poured kerosene over them. Mr. and Mrs. Yamashiro publicly testified that they had *"turned to God from idols"* and desired to *"serve the living and true God"* (1 Thessalonians 1:9). Mr. Yamashiro lit a match and tossed it onto the pile of idols. While the flames reached high into the sky, a man passed by and said, "What are you Baptists doing now?" (To people in a country steeped in heathenism, anything the Baptists did was always very strange.) Before Don could respond, Mr. Yamashiro said, "I have served these idols all my life, and they have never helped me in any way! I have found the true and living God, and I no longer need idols." His testimony for the Lord spoke louder and more powerfully than anything Don could have said.

At every service Don attended at Senri Newtown, he could count on seeing the Yamashiros. The joy of the Lord overflowed from Mr. Yamashiro. He was smiling every time Don saw him, and he always had a testimony of something God had done for him, someone he had led to the Lord, or of a specific prayer God had answered. He even became one of the first deacons in the church.

Years later, while walking up a hill to a church service, Mr. Yamashiro had a heart attack and went to be with the Lord at the ripe age of ninety-six. How good God had been to put faithful members like him into Don's life. Truly he was a brand plucked from the burning. From Shinto priest to Baptist deacon, his transformation was a miracle of the gospel.

Ishigoro and Elizabeth Whewell

A novice when it came to preaching in Japanese, Don jumped at any opportunity to hear someone preach in the language. On one occasion, a missionary friend, Vern Chandler, invited Don to hear a Japanese preacher named Ishigoro. Many of the Japanese preachers Don had heard used very little Scripture, spoke rapidly, and were difficult to comprehend, but when Ishigoro read Scripture, he did so slowly and distinctly. For the first time, Don could understand, and he followed the message carefully with great interest. As the message came to a close, God spoke to Don's heart: "This is the way you should preach in Japanese."

Don believed preaching should always be delivered in a way that people could understand and apply. The very essence of preaching is communication, so despite how much a preacher may know or say, if the people cannot comprehend the message, there is no real communication.

After hearing Ishigoro, Don decided that if God would use Senri Newtown Baptist Church to raise up future pastors, he wanted this man to teach them the practice of clear, biblical preaching. With the church's first anniversary service just around the corner, Don invited Ishigoro to preach for their church.

Ishigoro had been converted and discipled by an independent missionary named Elizabeth Whewell, who had been in Japan before World War II but had to return to the States during the war. Mrs. Whewell's church and ministry in Japan was called the Mino Mission. Through it, she discipled her Japanese converts so biblically that when she returned to Japan after the war, all of her previous converts were dead. They had refused to participate in the idol worship of bowing to the emperor and were martyred for their faith in Christ.

Some of the missionaries who were forced to leave Japan after the war made plans to return, and nearly all of them did so under the sponsorship of the national church of Japan—a group that forced the missionaries to conform to Japanese state requirements for churches. Mrs. Whewell refused to compromise with this state-controlled arrangement and determined to return to Japan another way, although many missionaries told her it would be impossible to enter the country on her own.

When Mrs. Whewell landed in Yokama, she heard an announcement over the public address system calling her to report to a specific office. Everyone was sure she would be detained and sent back to America. But God had other plans. When she reached the office, two Japanese soldiers bowed and courteously escorted her to a limousine, which brought her directly to the office of General Douglas MacArthur, with whom she had corresponded during the allied occupation of Japan. He'd heard about her situation and had obtained papers for her to serve in Japan as a missionary apart from the sponsorship of the liberal church.

This woman had experienced God's provision and protection in an amazing way. Her love for the Japanese people was immense. It was after her return to Japan that she reached and discipled Ishigoro.

When Don contacted Ishigoro about preaching, the Japanese man replied that he did not go anywhere without Mrs. Whewell's permission. This didn't sit well with Don. While he knew Mrs. Whewell was likely just trying to protect her impressionable converts from unhealthy affiliations, he didn't want to ask her for "permission" to have Ishigoro preach. But Don truly believed that Ishigoro would help the church, so he set his pride aside and made the phone call. To Don's delight, Mrs. Whewell agreed, and the anniversary service was tremendous. The church had 125 people in attendance that day, and several people came to Christ as Saviour.

You Can Preach in Japanese

Don had come to depend on Keita Takagi's help to preach God's Word to the Japanese, and he had all but forgotten Keita's original plan was to return to seminary after several months of partnering with Don. In early June of Senri Newtown's first year, Keita told Don that he would be leaving in August to return to America.

Don tried his best to persuade Keita to stay. He reminded Keita about the wonderful things God was doing through their work together—the souls that were being saved weekly, the new believers being baptized monthly, and the young people they were training to serve the Lord. But Keita was resolute. He knew God wanted him to return to seminary. And addressing the core of Don's deep anxiety he said, "You can preach in Japanese!"

ELEVEN—THE LORD STRETCHED

Don recalled the miserable failure that had been his first attempt to preach in Japanese, but it had been many months, and since then he'd been immersed in the Japanese culture, so he had a little more familiarity with the language. Don asked Keita to pray that God would allow him to preach in a way the people could actually understand.

With the help of his Japanese teacher, who came to the house three days a week, Don began to prepare messages in Japanese. It took him over forty hours to create one message.

On July 11, 1966, Don planned his second attempt to preach in Japanese. That Sunday came quickly, and Don was nervous. He begged God to help him make sense to these people. With the looming departure of Keita, he knew he didn't have much time to grow in the skill of Japanese preaching.

The room was filled that morning, and Don did not notice until the middle of his message that his teacher, Miss Sato, was in the congregation. He'd told her he was going to be preaching in Japanese so she had come to hear him, although she was a devout Buddhist. She sat studiously listening to every word. She did not trust Christ that morning, but at their next lesson she praised Don on his excellent pronunciation and grammar and the overall proficiency of the message.

Though it meant much to Don that his teacher was pleased with his progress, it meant more to know that God used his message to bring two souls to the Saviour. That Sunday changed everything. God infused Don with a new confidence, and from that day forward, he preached at least one new message each week in Japanese.

During this time, God was working mightily on two fronts: He was working at Senri Newtown Baptist Church but also in the hearts of the Sisk family. Don, Virginia, Renee, and Tim were growing in grace and experiencing the joy and blessings of God in ways they never dreamed.

Don often felt like Abraham's servant, Eliezer, who was required to express faith in seeking a bride for Isaac. In Genesis 24, as God intervened with providential circumstances, the servant recounted, "...*I being in the way, the Lord led me...*" (Genesis 24:27).

An intricate, marvelous, miraculous story had unfolded at Senri Newtown, and Don knew there was no way to explain what was happening apart from God. They were simply exactly where He wanted them to be and doing exactly what he wanted them to do. In His providence God chose to do a miraculous work through this family and in this church. Don knew they were simply "in the way" and, "the Lord led" them. And God was only beginning to fulfill the desires of Don's heart.

Twelve
THE LORD ENLARGED

Spring 1967–Autumn 1968

It was a blessing to the Sisks to see so many young people saved in the early days of Senri Newtown Baptist Church. Immediately, the Sisks began training them to further the kingdom of Christ and plugging them into areas of service. Discipleship was a high priority, for Don knew how important it was to ground new Christians in the truth of God's Word.

Keita Takagi's discipleship program, which originated from one he had taken in America, proved a critical tool in helping the new believers to become rooted and grounded in Christ. Don was thankful that someone had invested into Keita's life so he could advance the gospel and help Christians in Japan. It was full-circle discipleship at its finest—a working model of 2 Timothy 2:2: *"And the things that thou hast heard of me among many witnesses, the same commit thou to faithful men, who shall be able to teach others also."*

A Desire to Train Others for Ministry

Once the new converts began serving in various areas of ministry, Don watched in amazement at the tremendous growth they experienced. Within a year of their salvation, six young people—two college graduates, two high school graduates, and two high school students—had committed their lives to full-time Christian service.

One of the first young men to make this decision had graduated from a university in Japan as well as an art school in France. Even with all this schooling behind him, he still wanted to go to Bible college. He found a Bible college similar in doctrine and studied there for yet another four years.

While the young man learned many good things at Bible college, he also learned doctrine and philosophy that was very different from what Don believed and had taught. Don's first clue was when the young man returned home and printed the five points of Calvinism in the church bulletin.

As Don began thinking of the others who had surrendered their lives to the Lord, he was fearful to send them to similar training, lest they also be exposed to errant doctrine or philosophy. He determined that, if God would let him, he would start an institution for Japanese Christians desiring to train for ministry. Don began praying earnestly for the Lord to meet this need.

A Small Room and a Few Students

The Sisks were still working closely with the other BIMI missionaries who had welcomed them to Japan. David Marcum, who had gone to Japan eight months before the Sisks, and Ron White, who had only been in Japan two weeks when the Sisks arrived, were both working with a church in Nishinomiya, and both were also interested in and supportive of the work the Sisks had started. An additional BIMI missionary the Sisks had met in Japan was Leland Lanier.

After much prayer, Don decided to approach these men with his vision for a Bible institute for those who felt called into ministry. They were thrilled with the idea and committed to help in whatever way they could.

Don began compiling material and searching for a room they could use. He found an apartment complex in an older part of the city near the church with an upstairs room no larger than the average area rug—measuring only 6'x9'. In it was a long table with rectangular cushions, *zabutons,* surrounding it. Although the conditions were not optimal, Don sensed that time was fleeting. He rented the room and decided to begin immediately.

April 1967 brought the first day of training with three students in attendance: two young men, Ogawa and Uehara (who were both college graduates) and a young lady, Hiraoka (a recent high school graduate). A few weeks into the training, Omote, a young man from Ron White's ministry, joined.

Classes were held from 8:00 AM until 12:00 PM every Monday, Wednesday, and Friday. Their four subjects—Introduction to the New Testament, Introduction to the Old Testament, Baptist Doctrine and History, and How to Work for Christ—were each taught by one of the four missionaries. The students were passionate about their studies and progressed quickly.

God was changing lives every day, and at times the missionaries had to stop and catch their breath to keep up with all that He was doing. Within a matter of months, others became interested in joining the training institute. That summer at Bible camp, ten young people committed their lives to serve the Lord in full-time ministry, and three entered the institute the following fall.

Beginning a Bible College

By April of 1968, the missionaries realized they had a problem: there were more students wanting to train for ministry than there were space or materials. It had become clear they needed something larger than a training institute; they needed to start a Bible college.

The four missionaries set their energies to the task and soon had curriculum purchased, a doctrinal statement chosen, and a philosophy for the college formed. The doctrinal statement was taken from BIMI, and the philosophy was that all who taught in the institute would be men involved in evangelism and church planting and that all who came to the school would be interested in full-time Christian service.

With the foundation of the school established, the question of location was next on the list. God had temporarily provided a larger room, but after the first two years, there was a definite need for a place the students could stay overnight. The Sisks were still renting a home in Ashiya at the time, and there were several houses in the area similar to theirs. They ended up renting two more houses from their landlord. One was used for the girls' dormitory and classrooms, and the other for the men's dormitory and cafeteria.

The third year of the school began with thirteen students, and by this time the Lord had brought Sarah Lewis, a single missionary, to work in the field alongside the Sisks. She lived with the lady students in the dormitory, and the Lord used her greatly in their lives.

God was at work in ways the Sisks never imagined, and the devil was working overtime to destroy their efforts. They had very little support, and expenses were growing larger by the day. Most of the young people worked part-time jobs to help pay for their meals and contribute to the rent, but for school to continue operating, the Sisks needed the Lord to provide in a miraculous way.

Each of the missionaries were already contributing monthly to the school. There were also a few churches that began supporting the Bible college from America. In 1968, the Lord met the need in a wonderful way when a military church was started on the island of Okinawa. This church, the Maranatha Baptist Church, began giving generously to the school. Several of the military men who were members of this church began helping the Japanese students financially as well. Thus, the school was able to continue.

TWELVE—THE LORD ENLARGED

A New Location

Don's busiest season of ministry was just around the corner. Each of the churches started by the missionaries was growing, and God was calling people into full-time ministry on a regular basis. Dave Marcum and Ron White went on furloughs at the same time, which placed a greater load on Don's shoulders. He was responsible for all of the daily teaching and administration of the college in addition to pastoring the church in Senri Newtown. Don later realized he should have sought help and delegated some of his responsibilities, but at the time, it was just a matter of doing what he knew best. In spite of his limited wisdom, God was faithful through it all, and the work continued to prosper.

While Ron and Dave were on furlough, George King, a good friend and a missionary with Baptist Bible Fellowship International, came to visit Don regarding a location God had placed on his heart for the Bible college.

He asked Don to travel with him to the city of Akashi, about thirty-five miles away. A missions organization owned a few buildings there, but none were in use. George and Don arrived at the site to find half an acre of land with a church building and two homes—all vacant—and with enough additional land to build a small school building. Don walked the property in awe at how perfect it seemed for their needs.

The asking price for the property was $60,000, and Don's heart sank at this figure. In the past three years he had barely been able to raise $10,000 for land for the church, and this was the only cash the church had on hand. Raising six times that much money seemed impossible, but as Don took another look at the property, God impressed upon his heart to keep investigating.

Back home, Don contacted the Japanese man in charge of the property, who met with Don personally. Together they visited the property once again, and the property manager told Don the buildings had been built by the Slavic Oriental Mission but had never been used for their intended ministry purpose. The mission was currently pulling operations out of Japan and moving into Korea. He explained that while the owners were reluctant to lower the price, they were also desperate to sell the property.

Don began to pray earnestly and focused on raising money for this much-needed resource. He wrote letters to everyone he knew, including Ron and Dave, who were still in the States. Both men were enthusiastic about the possibility and began praying as well. Several weeks passed with no response. The ministry was still sitting on a meager $10,000. Don was out of ideas, so he called his missions director, Dr. Freeny, and asked him to join the prayer efforts.

Don felt certain that God had led him to this property but was disappointed that He had not yet provided.

He had proposed to the property manager that they put a down payment of $10,000 on the property and pay the balance over a five-year term, but the mission leaders declined, needing cash upfront to begin operations in Korea. Again, Don asked God for the money, but nothing came in.

One evening Don took his son Tim, now nine years old, to look at the property. That night, father and son knelt together and prayed fervently for God to provide.

Several days later, Don received a phone call from Dr. Lynn Jones, the executive director of the Slavic Oriental Missions. He had just recently arrived in Japan, had been told about Don's proposal, and wanted to meet Don.

A few days later, Don was sitting in his home with Dr. Jones as Mrs. Sisk served tea and cookies. Don thought the visit was merely a courtesy to say thanks for his interest in the property. But Dr. Jones asked to see the buildings the Sisks were renting and meet some of the students who were currently enrolled in the Bible college. Don took him to their meager campus and shared his vision for their future in ministry and ministry training.

As they returned to the house, Dr. Jones had tears in his eyes. He told Don that in his briefcase was a contract he'd intended to sign with an electric company for the sale of the property. But that morning he had awoken with an uneasy feeling. As he read his Bible it was almost as if God was telling him, "Here's a Christian organization that needs to use this property I gave you for My work, and you're selling it to an electric company." Dr. Jones continued, "Don, this is the worst business deal I ever made in my life, but I'm going to sell you the property for $10,000 down. We'll give you five years to pay for the rest, and there won't be any interest."

Don could not believe his ears. He was so elated by the news, he didn't know how to respond. With his head spinning and his heart overwhelmed, he thanked Dr. Jones and rushed to tell Virginia that God had provided yet again.

Kansai Independent Baptist Bible School

Don immediately contacted Dave and Ron and shared the news. They began working together on an agreement for living arrangements and finances. It was decided that the Sisks would live in one house on the property, and the Marcums would live in the other. Excluding Ron from the rent, they divided the payments into three parts for each of the men to contribute.

Don also began thinking about possibly starting a new church. With a church building situated between the two houses on the property, it was only logical that they should start a new church in Akashi.

Don took the Bible school students out to see the property for the first time. They looked with wonder at how God had blessed them. With enthusiasm they met together in the building each day to pray and thank God. They began dreaming about what would eventually be done on that property. The possibilities seemed endless.

By the time Ron and Dave returned to Japan, they had been able to raise and borrow enough money to build the Bible school building. Although this increased their debt, it was necessary before schooling could take place. This building was constructed within a matter of months, and by 1970, the Kansai Independent Baptist Bible School had a new home.

A New Church and a Growing Vision

In October of 1968, the Sisks celebrated the planting of a new church: Grace Baptist Church of Akashi. It had only been four years since they had started their first church, and in that short time they had seen phenomenal growth. God had blessed in every area of the work. The most rewarding part of God's work was the solidification of the new believers in Senri Newtown. It was amazing how quickly the young converts were growing and maturing in the Lord. Their acceptance of responsibility and their expression of great faith was an encouragement to the Sisks.

This season was one of watching God bless faith. It has been said that for a child to fully embrace the faith of his parents, he must see those parents express at least one act of courageous, radical, obedient faith. Perhaps this was the very season of life that solidified the faith of Renee and Tim during their formational years. They were able to watch and take part as their parents endured struggles, embraced dependence upon God, served with endurance, and saw the Lord intervene in undeniable ways.

The Sisks had been able to learn Japanese, plant two growing churches, and were seeing the fruit of young people's being saved and surrendering their lives for full-time ministry, a Bible college established to train future Japanese Christian leaders, and a new property provided on which a new college building had been constructed. Along the way, God sustained and met every need. His hand was evident every day in every way.

Prior to these days of blessing, the Sisks had travelled through some valleys. The dark, lonely days preceding made them enjoy the mountain top sunshine that much more. Everywhere they looked they saw God's blessings, and they were truly grateful.

And yet, even in the midst of the blessings, God led them into another valley.

Thirteen

THE LORD DISRUPTED

Autumn 1967– Spring 1968

Phone calls from America were a rare occurrence. Due to the expense, the call usually held urgent or distressing news. Such was the case in October of 1967 when Don received a call from his dad. Through tears, he relayed sad news, "Son, Mom is dying. She really hopes to see you before she goes to Heaven."

With an ocean between them, Don tried his best to comfort his father. He promised to do everything in his power to make it home before his mother passed away. As he hung up the phone, he wept—partially from the sadness of the news and partially because he had no idea how he could possibly afford a trip back to the States.

With a new church needing Don's direction, the timing was not good for an absence. So Don and Virginia began praying and considering what would be best. Other missionaries offered to assist with the ministry, but after much prayer Don felt the Japanese Christians were ready to do the job in his absence. He approached Sorogo Ogawa about serving as interim pastor and after talking to the church family and to Sogoro, the church accepted him as their pastor until the Sisks' return.

So just two and a half years after arriving in Japan, the Sisks boarded a plane back to America. They flew through Los Angeles and then to Phoenix to visit with their pastor, David Brown, who had resigned from their sending church in Illinois and accepted the pastorate of a church in Phoenix. They stayed at his home for a few days, and Don preached in three churches that Sunday morning. It seemed the longest day of his life. He was feeling desperate to get to his mom before she died.

Saying Goodbye to Mom

From Phoenix, the Sisks continued to Illinois, arriving in Harvey and staying with friends for several days while near their family. By this time, Don's mother was in the hospital and growing weaker with every passing day. Don visited with her in the hospital every day. She often took his hand in hers and reminded him that she was going to Heaven soon. Don's dad would sit by her bedside with tears in his eyes and say, "Son, I wish it could be me going and not her."

Earl Sr. had been saved at the age of fifty-seven, and the last years of Earl and Beulah's marriage had been spent growing in God's grace, serving Him, and loving each other more deeply. They'd attended church together faithfully, read the Bible, prayed, and simply had a wonderful life in their final days. In light of their earlier life and his dad's alcoholism, Don rejoiced in the power of the gospel and wonderful changes that God's grace had produced.

On November 29, Don received a call from his dad. His mother was fading quickly. Don rushed to the hospital as quickly as he could, but by the time he arrived, his mom was already in Heaven.

Don was thankful for the final days God had given him with his mother, and he worked with his siblings to make arrangements for the funeral. It was his mom's desire to be buried in Nortonville, Kentucky, her longtime home, so they held her funeral service at Nortonville's New Salem Baptist Church and buried their mother in the New Salem Cemetery. The day was solemn in many ways. Don reflected on his mom's life, considering the difficulties she'd endured and the patience and kindness she'd unwaveringly displayed. Her heart was exceptional, and Don was deeply grateful for the wonderful lady God had given him for a mother. Her influence on his life was profound.

Answers to Prayer and Visits with Friends

Don's sister, Francis, who lived in Chicago, made the trip back to Nortonville with the Sisks. On the way, Don had the wonderful opportunity to share the gospel with her and see her trust Christ as her Saviour. He had trusted from the beginning that God had a plan in taking his mother, but with the salvation of his sister, Don became more thankful for God's providence. Francis was the last of his family to be saved, which was an answer to a prayer of Don's heart since his own salvation at age sixteen.

After the funeral, the Sisks were out of money and needed a place to stay. God touched the hearts of Richard and Kay Griffin, good friends from Calvary Baptist Church in Harvey, and they opened their home to the family for several days. The Griffins had a split-level home with complete living spaces on both levels, and they gave the Sisk family the entire lower level. It was this generosity that made their visit to the states affordable.

While in Kentucky, Don visited Providence Baptist where they had once served. After he'd seen many old friends, Don was reminded of

Jimmy, the retired veteran who had sent the two $100 checks at just the right time. Don made his way to Jimmy's house to say thank you.

Jimmy's mother answered the door, and when he asked for Jimmy, she bowed her head and began to weep.

"Don, didn't anyone tell you?" she said. "Jimmy went to be with the Lord several months ago."

When Don heard the date that Jimmy passed away, he realized it had happened just two short weeks after he'd written the checks for the church in Japan. By the time Don had received the checks, Jimmy was already rejoicing in Heaven.

Jimmy had been sensitive to the Lord's prompting in his life, and as a result, he impacted many for Christ before he went to Heaven. Spiritual investments into eternity can only bring great dividends. As the years of Don's ministry continued to unfold, He never forgot the way that God used Jimmy to answer a desperate prayer.

Would Jesus Save an Old Man Like Me?

During their short time in America, the Sisks found themselves thinking about the work in Japan and wishing they were back "home." Not long after their arrival, Don received a letter from Sogoro Ogawa with more sad news: "*Ojisan* ('granddad') went to heaven just the other day." Don wept as he read the words and reflected on meeting a man named Mr. Kitanaka who had come to mean so much to him.

In 1966, when Senri Newtown Baptist Church was still brand new, a woman approached Don after a service and said, "*Sensei* ('teacher') my father is coming to visit us. He is seventy-six years old. As far as I know, he has never heard about Jesus Christ. Would you come and tell my father about Jesus Christ? I believe if you tell him, he will be saved."

This woman had only been saved a few weeks, yet her zeal for Christ was strong. Don could not help but admire her faith in the power of the gospel. He told her he'd be delighted to come. He visited her house that Thursday night with Keita and together they met her father, who was sitting at a little table called a *kotatsu*. They all gathered around the table, drank green tea, and ate oranges and other fruit.

It is Japanese custom to share much light conversation before getting to the real reason for a visit; skipping this small talk is considered rude. For Don, whose heart was aching to share the gospel, the wait through the opening conversation was agonizing. But eventually the conversation turned, and Don began to tell Mr. Kitanaka about Jesus Christ. From the time he began, the man fastened his eyes on Don with intensity. The only word he said during the entire salvation story was "*Hai*." ("I'm listening, go ahead.")

Don read Scripture that explained the vicarious suffering of Christ and shared how Jesus died for all of his sins. Mr. Kitanaka kept repeating "*Hai*," so Don explained how Jesus' body was taken from the cross and buried in the tomb. Then Don said, "But on Sunday morning when they went to look for the body of Jesus at the tomb, there was nobody there. He had been resurrected from the grave."

This was more than Mr. Kitanaka could comprehend. His eyes wide open and full of awe, he said, "*Sensei*, is this a real story?"

Don replied, "Oh, yes, Mr. Kitanaka, this is a real story. And, not only did Jesus really suffer, bleed, and die on the cross to be buried and resurrected from the grave, but He is also really here in this room with us tonight. If you would be willing to bow your head right now and confess that you are a sinner on your way to Hell, Jesus Christ would come into your heart and save you from all of your sin."

In Don's experience of telling Japanese people of the gospel of Jesus, he had learned it sometimes took many months before they would willingly admit they were sinful and needed a Saviour. It was unusual that Mr. Kitanaka realized his sin and took responsibility for it in just one sitting. But with tears welling in his eyes he said, "*Sensei*, do you think He would save an old man like me?"

Don smiled. "Sir, I believe you are just the kind of man He came to die for."

They bowed their heads, and Don led Mr. Kitanaka in a sinner's prayer. As he finished praying, tears of joy ran down his wrinkled cheeks, and Don could see a tremendous burden had been lifted from his soul. They rejoiced together, and Don taught him the song "Amazing Grace." Don shared verses on assurance, and just a few days later, Mr. Kitanaka followed Jesus in believer's baptism. Over time, the two men became good friends.

On the Sunday before Don and his family returned to America, Don had gone to visit the church one last time and as he parked the car, he saw Mr. Kitanaka standing in front of the building. As soon as he saw Don, Mr. Kitanaka began to bow, the respectful equivalent of shaking hands in America. Don bowed in return.

Mr. Kitanaka laid a hand on Don's shoulder and said, "*Sensei*, you came a long way from America just to tell me about Jesus. From the depth of my heart, I want to thank you."

Don was overwhelmed by this man's gratitude. He considered it a great privilege to tell literally thousands of Japanese people about Jesus in such a short time. He thanked God for many they had seen saved. As he looked into the eyes of this joyful old man, he couldn't help but think, "If Mr. Kitanaka was the only one saved—the only reason God brought us to Japan—that would have been worth it all."

Senri Newtown Baptist Church held a Christian funeral for Mr. Kitanaka and preached the gospel to those present. Many accepted Christ, and Don rejoiced in the work that was going forward in his absence. He wished he'd had the opportunity to say goodbye to Mr. Kitanaka but looked forward to the day they would be reunited in Heaven. Don imagined what it would be like to see him in eternity. He envisioned the man placing his hand on Don's shoulder and thanking him for giving him the good news of Jesus. Then he imagined him thanking every person who helped support Don and Virginia as missionaries to Japan.

As Don folded the letter from the interim pastor and placed it in his Bible, he considered what a wonderful place Heaven would be.

Amazing Provision in America

Without the funds to immediately return to Japan, the Sisks had to stay in America several months to raise additional support. During this time God taught them much. Renee attended a large high school where she was completely miserable for several days. It was difficult re-adjusting to American life, but eventually she acclimated and found her stride. Tim was in the first grade, and he cried every day on his way to school. As he walked home each day with Virginia, he would say over and over again, "I don't like this place. I want to go back home."

Tim adjusted soon enough, and the Sisks were delighted to see that God had anchored their children's hearts in Japan. They were thrilled to hear Renee and Tim refer to Japan as "home" and were grateful for the love God had given them for the Japanese people.

Although it was wonderful to be back in America and see old friends, the Sisk's hearts were in Japan. They applied themselves to raising funds for the return trip, and surprisingly, doors began opening all over the country. Without even making phone calls, somehow word spread. Within a few weeks, Don had booked a full schedule of preaching in revival meetings, visiting supporting churches, attending missions conferences, and presenting their work in new churches. The Sisks desperately needed additional support for their work in Japan, and it quickly became clear that God had planned this trip to meet that need.

By the time they returned to Japan in June, their support had increased significantly, giving them the financial support that they should have had when they originally left the States. God not only met their need, He exceeded their expectations and provided wonderfully for the new church in Senri Newtown, and for the Bible school.

During one meeting where Don was speaking, Dr. Freeny approached him and said, "BIMI has missionaries in the Islands, in Nicaragua, and a few in Mexico, but the only Asian country in which we are involved is Japan. Would you visit some of the other Asian countries and pray about the possibility of becoming a director or a representative for BIMI?" Don thanked him for the opportunity, but declined; he had no aspirations beyond getting back to the work in Japan. But with that conversation a seed was planted.

After a few months, the American furlough came to a close and the Sisks reflected on all God had done during the short time. Although they still grieved the loss of their mother and grandmother, Don's sister had accepted Christ, money was provided for their work in Japan, and lifetime providential friendships were formed. A trip that had begun as an interruption turned out to be a critical blessing and God's providential provision for their work. Don was reminded that God was in control, and His work had only just begun. The Sisk family was reminded that joy was not found in a geographic location, but in the spiritual center of God's perfect will. God knew their needs and could be trusted to abundantly provide in the right way, at the right time.

The Sisks had discovered in a marvelous way that God's disruptions are often God's provisions. Revived and refreshed for the work ahead, they boarded a plane back to Japan with great anticipation of what God would do in the days ahead.

Fourteen

THE LORD SUSTAINED

1968–1970

After several months of renewal in America, the Sisks were excited to finally return to the country they now considered home. On furlough they had purchased a washer and dryer, bedroom furniture, a living room set, and other household items to fit the needs of their growing family. Through BIMI they were able to ship these things to Japan at no cost. They were excited to be returning and to soon be moving to the new property in Akashi.

Shortly after arriving back in Japan in mid-1968, it became obvious to Don that his goal to plant an indigenous church was coming to fruition. Pastor Ogawa had been accepted by the people of Senri Newtown Baptist Church and had done a fabulous job as interim pastor, growing in wisdom and spiritual maturity during Don's absence.

Pastor Ogawa graciously stepped down from the temporary position upon Don's return, insisting that Don resume preaching once again. Don felt that sharing the preaching responsibilities would be best, because He wanted Pastor Ogawa to continue his leadership in the church.

Don was thankful the church had continued to grow and flourish. People were being saved on a weekly basis, and the new believers were growing in their commitment to the Lord in every area. Gradually, the church was growing stronger financially as well—a critical aspect of eventually becoming an indigenous church.

Pastor Ogawa's Marriage

Considering the church's growth and Pastor Ogawa's godly leadership, Don knew he would soon be leaving the church plant to start another work for the Lord. It was clear that Pastor Ogawa was ready for this responsibility, and the two men began talking through the transition.

Don's only concern was that Sogoro was unmarried, and with the number of single young ladies in the church, it would not be wise for him to become pastor until he was married. When he shared this concern with Sogoro, the younger man asked, "Teacher, which girl should I marry?" Don was shocked at the innocence and sincerity of his question. Gathering his thoughts quickly, he promised Sogoro that he and Virginia would pray about it and talk with him at a later time.

In actuality, Sogoro's question peeled back another layer of understanding into the Japanese culture for Don. Japanese young people deeply respect their elders and allow them great entrance into their decision making. Sogoro was extending to Don, as his spiritual mentor, the same respect he would to a grandfather.

Don and Virginia did pray for Sogoro. Through prayer, a young lady named Sachiko Hiraoka came to mind. She was a dedicated Christian lady who had been saved early in their ministry. She served faithfully at the church as a Sunday school teacher and worked diligently as a Bible school student. Virginia had been able to mentor Sachiko one on one sometime previously, and the young woman's servant's heart and increasing spiritual maturity had been a blessing to her.

Don suggested to Sogoro that Sachiko might make a wonderful wife, if the Lord were to confirm an interest in his heart. Sogoro's response was hard to read—neither positive nor negative, but definitely thoughtful. Within a few days Don noticed that Sogoro and Sachiko were talking more frequently, and soon after, they began to date and fell in love. After a time of proving God's will, the couple became engaged, wedding plans were made, and Don was privileged to perform his first wedding in Japan.

What began with a young college student crashing a church service to practice his English had blossomed into more than Don could have ever imagined. It was a joy to see this couple come to Christ, grow in their faith, prepare for ministry, fall in love, and begin a new family. For many years now, Pastor Ogawa and Sachiko have faithfully served the church family at Senri Newtown Baptist Church. Don and Virginia grew to consider the Ogawas some of their dearest friends.

Renee Goes to College

The year was 1970, and God was working mightily in the lives of the Japanese people within reach of the Sisks. Great things were happening in the ministry, and new missionaries were coming to the field on a regular basis. Young people were committing their lives to full-time Christian ministry, and the Bible school was flourishing. As the year wound toward autumn, in the midst of all of these blessings, the Sisks faced a life change that hit them like a ton of bricks: their oldest child was going to college.

Renee was to return to America, where she planned to attend Tennessee Temple University in Chattanooga, Tennessee. This was one of the most difficult things the Sisks faced while on the field. Renee was their first child to leave home, and they were novices at how to prepare themselves, much less Renee, for the dramatic emotions and change this brought into their lives. Renee would make the long trip from Osaka to Tokyo, then from Tokyo to America all alone. While Don wished that he and Virginia could accompany her, the financial demand was too great. And being the independent young woman she was, Renee assured her parents she would be fine.

The day of Renee's departure came all too quickly. The Sisks placed her small suitcase in their van and drove to the Osaka airport. As the time came to say goodbye, the weight of the moment finally sank in, and Don said, "I think I'm going to get a ticket and at least go with you to Tokyo." Renee calmed his fears and explained it would be a ludicrous waste of money. She confidently told her dad, "I'm grown, and I can take care of it."

This was indeed the case. Renee would have no problem navigating her way to America, but Don was having a hard time letting her go. Excited about her future and with very few tears of her own, Renee said goodbye, stepped on the plane, and waved cheerfully to her family.

By the time the Sisks had arrived back in Akashi, Renee had landed in Tokyo and the reality of leaving home had begun to sink in. Her brave façade had finally burst, and she called her parents weeping, which made Virginia cry as well. Virginia handed the phone to Don and said, "You talk with her. I don't know what to say."

That conversation was one of the most difficult Don ever had. Renee pleaded with her father to let her come home. She told him she didn't want to leave her family and friends.

Don's emotions screamed at him to give in. He longed to tell her, "Of course you can come home!" Only by God's grace and Holy Spirit was he able to encourage her to continue on to the States. He reminded her that they had prayed about the decision and assured her it was God's will for her to go to college.

After ten or fifteen minutes, Renee's spirit calmed, and her heart settled enough for her to admit, "I know this is what God wants. I shouldn't have said what I said."

As Don hung up the phone, he looked at his wife and said, "We'd better pray." Together, they prayed for Renee and for themselves. As they prayed, the phone rang again. Don looked at Virginia and said, "If that's her and she wants to come home, I don't think I can tell her no this time." Fortunately, it wasn't Renee.

Several hours later, Renee called her parents from Hawaii and assured them her childhood days were over. It wasn't long before she was excelling at college and paying much of her bill through the work scholarship program. She worked long, hard hours, but she learned much, matured on many levels, and made wonderful memories.

The Power of Patience and Prayer

By October of 1970, plans were underway for a new church plant, support was sufficient, and the Bible school was growing in attendance. Despite these blessings, Don felt something was missing in his life and work, but what it was he didn't fully understand.

After furlough, he had resumed his weekly routines in the work, but something had changed. He couldn't seem to regain his rhythm of daily life and ministry in Japan. His heart was in the right place, but still he struggled to feel in sync and to sense God moving as he had just a year before.

One day, as he studied God's Word, he contemplated the problem, searching his heart for what he might be doing wrong. God simply didn't seem to be moving and working in the same way He had before the furlough. And then in a moment of epiphany, the Lord revealed the problem: Don had lost his greatest prayer warrior—his mother.

Realizing the need for prayer support, Don sent out a simple prayer letter emphasizing the many blessings of God in the work in Japan. The Sisks had enough financial support, many new believers growing, and they had a better grasp of the language, but they were in significant need of prayer. He asked readers to consider taking his mother's place as their prayer warrior. In response, several people told Don that they would pray for him on regular basis. He was overjoyed and immediately sensed the prayers of those new warriors on their behalf.

Soon, though it seemed only a short time since the first service at Senri Newtown, God had already ordained another first service in their ministry. This time it was the Grace Baptist Church in Akashi, and the first service saw more than forty people in attendance, including the Bible School students. From the beginning, God blessed the new ministry. Grace Baptist Church did not have the same dramatic launch as Senri Newtown Baptist, but still God's hand was evident in specific and undeniable ways.

Spiritual Attacks Within the Ministry

For years, the BIMI missionaries in Japan had worked together and fellowshipped with joy and unity. All of that changed, however, for a short period in 1969 and 1970. In the midst of the unfolding ministries of the churches, the Bible school, and the Christian day camps, there was a period of time that was unpleasant for all of the missionaries in that region.

It was unclear how the dissension began, but whatever the cause, all the missionaries reacted in the flesh. A few issues arose with BIMI that were not nearly as important as they seemed at the time, and the end result of this disagreement was that Don felt it would be best to resign his position with the Bible school and continue his work in the church and other activities. The disagreement led to difficult months and, in some ways, years of strained relationships. But in the end, God's grace was bigger than the tension, and He worked in the heart of each missionary.

During this struggle, Don read a small book entitled, *Your Reactions are Showing* by J. Allan Petersen that convicted him of his own selfishness in the situation. After reading it, he repented of the bitterness that had grown in his heart. Peace and joy returned, and Don saw how he had begun to quench the work of God's Spirit in and through his life. He also recognized anew how masterful Satan was at distracting Christians with issues that would later prove to be petty and inconsequential. Since that time, whenever Satan has attempted to divide and hurt relationships in Don's life, he has tried to see the bigger, long-term perspective by asking, "Will this really be important twenty-five years from now?" By God's grace he determined to *respond* rather than *react* and to avoid being drawn into prideful, fleshly struggles among believers.

Perhaps this is why today, it is nearly impossible to find someone who knows Don Sisk who doesn't respect, love, and appreciate him, even if they disagree with him. He has determined to be a gracious, kind, joyful, forgiving man who holds no grudges and lets the Lord fight the battles that are truly worth fighting. He has a reputation for being a peacemaker, an encourager, and a strengthener of his brethren all over the world.

Another Opportunity in the States

Since the Sisks had been in Japan, it was rare to receive a phone call that did not force them to their knees in urgent prayer. This was the case when a deacon from their sending church, Calvary Baptist in Harvey, Illinois, called to announce that the church family had unanimously voted to ask the Sisks to return to America so Don could become their senior pastor.

Don believed he was where God wanted him to be in Japan, but at the same time, he wanted to be careful not to miss the leading and direction of God. Calvary Baptist Church was a wonderful place of ministry. The church had a beautiful building, a large congregation, and many positive opportunities for the gospel. Moreover, while Don deeply loved the people of Japan, he also loved his Calvary Baptist family, who had been there for him and his family on many occasions. His heart torn, Don spent many days searching his heart and asking God for guidance. Unable to come to a conclusion for several weeks, he finally asked his friend, Ron White, to come and pray with him after church one Sunday evening.

After the service that night, Don told Ron the story and asked him to pray that the Lord would show him what to do. Amazingly, as they got on their knees and began to pray, God's will became clear to Don in a way he had never experienced. As Ron closed his prayer, Don paused and said, "I don't understand it, but God just showed me without a doubt that it is not His will for me to be the pastor of Calvary Baptist Church."

Still not fully understanding God's ways, Don called Calvary Baptist and told the deacon he was honored at being asked to fill the position, but it was not God's will for his life. The church was disappointed, but Don never once questioned the decision. He held the promise of Proverbs 3:5–6 and believed God had directed his path as he had acknowledged Him.

When God Teaches the Teacher

The first year back in Japan after the Sisks' short furlough, brought with it many new experiences and much personal growth. In many ways, it wasn't what Don expected, but God was working greatly in the ministries and in the Sisks' lives.

In retrospect, Don sees this season as a teaching season. It was more about what God was doing *within* him, than what God was doing *through* him. That wasn't possible to see at the time, and like most men at that age, Don was more interested in visible fruit than internal, less-visible fruit.

He was so busy teaching *others* that he never really paused to consider how deeply God was teaching *him*.

In the thick of this season, it just felt that he was trudging forward through unexpected developments and life adjustments. While he didn't question God's will, he often questioned what God was doing. He couldn't see it then as clearly as he can now that it was a maturing time—a season when God was working more *deeply* than *visibly*. God knew the doors that He would open for the Sisks just around the corner, and He knew the work required to prepare Don to step through those open doors.

And yet, even in this season, there was a lot to be thankful for in family and ministry life. The new Japanese Christians were growing in devotion and fervor for the Lord. Both churches were developing wonderfully. Renee was enjoying college, Tim was in upper elementary school, and the Sisks looked to the future with anticipation of what God had in store.

Don looks back on these days with deep gratitude for what God did within him, as much as for what God was doing around him. Today it is clear, the deeper work of *teaching* his servant was critical for the future *reaching* that God would allow him to do.

Fifteen
THE LORD DIRECTED

1970–1972

Don was thirty-eight years old, and, though he was still young, the Lord had directed his life through seasons of faith and obedience down paths he never could have imagined. With every new day, Don found his heart for God growing deeper and his burden to influence others with the gospel growing stronger.

Recent changes in Don's weekly commitments allowed him to invest more time into the church at Akashi. As a result, the church began to flourish throughout the last months of 1970. Don was grateful for the blessings God brought and was pleased with how the church was growing.

Furlough in the States

The Sisks had now been in Japan for nearly seven years with only a short return to the States in late 1967. Don began to feel that he and his family needed a furlough, so he made plans for a trip home and a much-needed time of rest for the family. He spoke with Bill Griffin, a missionary involved in the church, about overseeing the work while they were away, and in June of 1971, Don, Virginia, and Tim boarded a plane to America.

In an effort to be accessible to Renee in college, they considered making Harvey, Illinois, their residence so they could attend their sending church, Calvary Baptist and still be within driving distance of Renee. But much had changed since they'd last attended Calvary. The church had recently appointed a new pastor whose doctrinal position was different than their own, which led the Sisks to begin praying about a new sending church.

Ultimately, they decided to ask Highland Park Baptist Church in Chattanooga to be their sending church. This worked out wonderfully for Renee because Highland Park Baptist was the home church of Tennessee Temple University. But it wasn't easy to transition to a different sending church. The Sisks had lifelong friends at Calvary Baptist, which made it difficult to leave. They continued their friendships with many of the church family, and to this day they still share wonderful relationships from those days.

Similar to their first furlough, this second trip to America was both refreshing and demanding. From the moment they landed until the day they went back to Japan, their schedule was booked solid with meetings. God opened many doors to present the work and preach to American Christians about global missions. During their travels, several people surrendered their lives to the mission field.

While speaking in various missions conferences, the Sisks often intersected with Dr. Freeny, the General Director of BIMI. Every time he saw Don he'd say, "We still need a Far Eastern Director and I feel you're the man for that position." It was difficult to think about this with so many other things going on, but Don finally promised he would pray about the need, and he committed to take time to visit other Asian countries when he was back in Japan.

Returning to Japan

The Sisks returned to Japan in 1972 to begin their third term. Their time in America had rekindled their hearts for the mission field, and they were eager to get back to God's work and God's people in Japan. But they returned to find that in their absence, the church in Akashi had suffered a large drop in attendance. Although interest in the church had previously been at an all time high, there was now little to no interest, and what remained was a struggling church and a small, discouraged group of Christians.

Resisting the temptation to also become discouraged, Don faithfully engaged in the work of rebuilding the church. In addition to the church at Akashi, he agreed to oversee the church of a friend in Tokyo who was home on furlough. Once each month he scheduled another man to preach at Akashi and boarded a train for Tokyo, where he preached, administered the Lord's Supper, baptized believers, and conducted a business meeting with the church family.

For a long season, he carried the weight of two ministries in two different regions, which spread him pretty thin. But God gave grace with each new day.

Papa is in Heaven

One year into his third term, Don received the urgent phone call from Renee, who cried as she told him she'd just learned that Earl Sr. had passed away.

Don's papa had a very difficult time on his own after his wife died. He had remarried a gracious woman but died suddenly of a heart attack, which was surprising because he was in good physical condition and had never suffered from heart problems.

The news hit Don hard. He grieved that both of his parents were now gone, but he rejoiced that they were reunited in Heaven. He thanked the Lord for the opportunity to see his father trust Christ as Saviour so many years earlier.

Don told Renee that he wasn't sure he would make it home for the funeral. Considering the expense and the fact that his mother had already passed, he didn't feel his presence was all that critical. But then Virginia reminded him that Papa had specifically asked Don to preach at his funeral. God placed a burden on Don's heart to keep that commitment.

Rather than ask others for help with the trip's expenses, he purchased the airfare with his credit card and determined to pay it off on a monthly basis. This bothered him, but he didn't feel that he had another reasonable option at the time.

Don felt that one of the reasons God led him to return for his dad's funeral was that many of Earl's unsaved friends would be attending. The funeral was held in Earl's hometown of Nortonville, at the New Salem Baptist Church, and Don had prepared a simple salvation message for the service. He told those in attendance that Papa had been saved when he was fifty-seven and the greatest regret of his life was that he had not accepted Christ sooner. He had only nineteen years of his life to live for the Lord, but he used them wisely and had been thankful for each one. Don told them that Earl had often said, "I am not all that I should be, but thank God, I am not what I used to be." (Most of the people at the funeral knew him before his salvation, and many nodded in agreement.) His dad would then finish with, "And I'm not what I'm going to be."

Don reminded those in attendance that Papa was aware that one day he would see the Lord, old things would pass away, and all things would become new. He included the gospel in this funeral message, and when he invited those who would right then trust Christ as their Saviour to raise their hands, several people responded. Don knew Papa would be grateful.

God Opens Another Door

The week after the funeral, Don visited Renee in Chattanooga and while there, he received a call from Dr. Freeny asking if he would come to BIMI headquarters. When Don arrived, the older man welcomed him and once again repeated the need for a Far East Director.

"I really believe God could wonderfully use you here in America to stir the hearts of people in the churches, to preach in mission conferences, Bible colleges, and to encourage people to go to Japan, Korea, the Philippines, and other places in Asia," Dr. Freeny said. "Consider how greatly this would multiply your ministry."

Dr. Freeny and other missionaries had mentioned this need many times, but for some reason this time was different. God began to deal with Don's heart about the position. It was an extremely difficult decision because Don saw himself as a missionary to Japan, not a missions director for the Far East. He promised Dr. Freeny he would pray about it and get back to him.

After returning to Japan, Don reluctantly began to discuss the opportunity with Virginia. She had always been supportive of God's leading in Don's life, and this time it was no different, but it was hard for her.

This particular decision was the one Virginia wrestled with and questioned the most. She expressed her support, but then made a statement that only served to make the issue heavier: "Don, you better be very careful. This is a huge decision." He acknowledged her warning, and knew in his heart that he had her full support and faith, regardless of how God led.

Surrendering to God's Call Yet Again

If the Sisks were going to make a transition, this was the appropriate time. God had laid the foundation in many ways. The church in Akashi was in the process of calling a new pastor named Hiraoka, an eager young man who had been saved at Senri Newtown Baptist Church. He and his wife were godly Christians, and Don and Virginia felt confident they would do well in Akashi. Don asked Hiraoka to come and preach for a month. The people responded well to him and later welcomed him as their new pastor.

During the transition, Don decided to work with Pastor Hiraoka for a few months. This gave him the opportunity both to seek the Lord's leading regarding the BIMI directorship position and to begin looking for another place to plant a church. The need for the gospel all around Japan was still so significant that Don was literally overwhelmed. It seemed the best place to plant a church in Japan, or the entire Asian region for that matter, was *everywhere*.

Don loved life in Japan and really had no desire to return to America. But what he was experiencing caught him off guard. For several years he had been focused on his work in one region and had done his best to bring the gospel and meet the immediate needs of those in a few cities. Now it seemed that God took blinders off his eyes. His heart was suddenly enlarged, and his vision and burden instantly grew greater.

It seemed *where* to start a church was not the issue; it was *whether* to start a church. God was increasingly stirring his heart toward a decision about the Far East Directorship.

Because Don still wasn't clear how God was leading, he didn't rush forward. He waited with a listening heart. He refused to take matters into his own hands or to force the circumstances to fit his script.

Instead, he chose to claim God's promises and to wait on God's clarity. He didn't see God's will as something he had to "find" quickly but something God would communicate clearly when He was ready. Listening to God can be an exercise of silence. When He seems to be saying nothing, that doesn't mean He isn't working. And to the listening heart and seeking soul, God does eventually speak. He always guides and directs with absolute clarity and certainty. He promises to order the steps of those who want to follow Him. Yet, preceding the clarity is always the agonizing wait.

For Don, waiting brought growing clarity until there was no denying God's direction. Through much prayer and consideration, and with a fresh step of renewed surrender to God, Don ultimately felt God was leading their family to return to America to become the Far East Director for BIMI.

He wrote Dr. Freeny a letter accepting the position but included a condition: "I am requesting that you view my acceptance of the position as temporary. I accept the position only with the understanding that I may relinquish it at any time and return to Japan."

Don did not believe this transition would be permanent. With the needs he saw all around him, he thought it would only be a short time before he returned to Japan to plant more churches.

Little did he know that God had other plans, and this would be the end of his resident missionary work in Japan. Nor did he anticipate the open doors and global opportunities for the gospel that God intended to open to him, so long as he kept patiently listening and obeying God's daily direction.

Sixteen

THE LORD EXPANDED

1973–1984

For the Sisk family, leaving Japan was more difficult than leaving America the first time seven years earlier. Leaving America had been trying in many ways, but their hearts had become so deeply knit to the Japanese people and their burden was so utterly consuming that when God asked them to leave Japan, it was devastating.

But the Sisks obeyed the leading of the Lord. With great sorrow, they made preparations to leave the people they had led to Christ and discipled in Japan. These Christians had become their spiritual family and close friends. Japan had been a wonderful home which they had never envisioned leaving. They thanked the Lord for the marvelous work He had done while they were there, and they hoped He would allow them to return.

Getting Settled in Chattanooga

In June of 1973, the family arrived in Chattanooga, Tennessee, to begin their work at the headquarters of BIMI. After several weeks of searching unsuccessfully for a home, they subleased an apartment from a widow who was planning to be away.

Houses were relatively inexpensive at the time, and eventually the Sisks purchased a newer home about thirty minutes from Highland Park Baptist Church and Tennessee Temple Christian Schools where Tim attended junior high and Renee was still attending college. The builder had only lived in the house for a year. It was a three-bedroom, 1,500 square foot house with a split foyer, and the asking price was only $21,500. They put $5,000 down and financed the rest.

With the help of a few friends, Don finished the basement and put in a fireplace. The house was comfortable and spacious, and Renee loved being able to spend her last year of college living at home.

Serving as Far East Director

Serving as Far East Director for BIMI was much like being a missionary. Directors were required to raise their own support, so Don and Virginia began to schedule meetings with their supporting churches to explain their position change and with new churches to raise additional support. Few of their churches dropped their support, and in a very short time, God provided the additional funds for Don to begin his work as a director in early 1974.

Within just six months, Don's schedule was full as God opened doors for him to preach and share his burden for missions. By the end of his first year his schedule was packed, and he had received more preaching invitations than he could possibly accept. He was privileged to speak at missions conferences and Christian colleges across the country. His goal was not to raise support for himself, but rather to kindle a fire in Christians' hearts for missions around the world. And God blessed his labor; in nearly every meeting, people surrendered their lives to be missionaries, and many surrendered specifically to go to fields in Asia.

The transition from active resident missionary to field director was not easy, but it was obvious that God had orchestrated the move. Strangely, though he was in the center of God's will, Don often struggled with a deep sense of dissatisfaction. He was delighted with the fruit of ministry unfolding around him, but he missed the personal relationships and heart connections he had experienced in working with people in Japan. Going from meeting to meeting didn't afford the same delight of developing close, discipling relationships.

Don would often come home from a conference and tell his wife, "We better not settle down too much. I don't think we're going to be here very long." They both longed for the personal connections they shared with new Christians when they were in Japan.

Missing Japan, Growing in the States

While the longing for Japan never completely left his heart, Don was grateful that the Lord helped his family re-adjust to life in the States. Tim loved attending school, and Virginia eventually made new friends and enjoyed her adult Bible class on Sundays at church. Highland Park Baptist Church was a thriving church with many opportunities for fellowship, and Virginia was soaking up her new Christian family.

Every summer, the Sisks returned to Japan for several weeks to visit different ministries. This was one of the great blessings of being the Far East Director and the highlight of their year. Each time they landed in Osaka, they felt like they were home again, and it never became easier to say goodbye and return to America. In addition to Japan, they also visited missionaries in Korea, the Philippines, and several other Asian countries.

After a few years, the Sisks realized that God would probably never send them back to Japan as resident missionaries. This realization brought a tremendous struggle as they had a difficult time letting go of their dream to return to Japan.

A Decade of Growing Influence

The Sisks served in ministry to the Far East from 1974 to 1984. Don was astounded at what God did during this season of his life. He had envisioned serving the remainder of his years as a missionary, but little did he know how God would use him to impact the hearts and lives of thousands of missionaries who would end up serving all over the world.

During these years as Far East Director, God sent many missionaries to the fields of the Philippines, Korea, Taiwan, Thailand, Japan, and other regions. Seeing young families surrender, prepare, raise support, train, and leave for the field became a core passion for Don. He was grateful that God would allow him to influence so many, inspiring them through His Word to care about the work of the gospel around the world.

At each conference or church service, Don was also privileged to use God's Word to challenge those American Christians who were *not* called to the mission field to be more generous and faithful in their missions giving to help those who *were* called. He desired that churches in America become stronger and more heavily invested into missions around the world, that more young people be enabled to get to the field sooner, and that those already in the field be sufficiently supported and encouraged by churches at home.

This was not a role Don could have foreseen, but after several years, he could see clearly that God had ordained it in his life. Just as the world needs missionaries, America needs those who biblically stir churches to greater participation in world evangelization. This passion has continued to grow in Don's heart to this very day. He has expended his life to inspire people to either go to the mission field or help those who will.

During this season, Don made many pastor friends and had the opportunity to speak in some of the great churches in America at the time. God opened doors for him to preach at places like Hyles-Anderson College, Bob Jones University, Tennessee Temple University, and others. He also had the privilege of being chosen to be the assistant moderator of the Southwide Baptist Fellowship. Don was continually surprised at each opportunity, and he was grateful that God would use him and give him increased influence—not to enlarge himself or his reputation, but to magnify Christ and challenge others to love and serve Him.

Over the years, the Lord used many books to help Don develop as a Christian and a leader. As a young preacher, he read *The Soul Winner's Fire* by Dr. John R. Rice, and it changed his life and his heart for the lost. Zig Ziglar's *See You at the Top* increased Don's desire to be an instrument of blessing to others. But one of the greatest books Don ever read outside his Bible was Oswald Sanders' *Spiritual Leadership*. In it, Sanders wrote, "You can get any thing you want, if you help enough people get what they want." Don began to see ministry in a whole new light as he understood this truth. It wasn't about getting what he wanted; it was about serving others and helping them become who God wanted them to be. Rather than just hosting missions conferences at other churches, he began to invest more deeply, desiring to help the pastor, encourage the pastor's wife, and strengthen the people in the church. Through the years, this single idea became a life philosophy that has compelled him to continually encourage others in the ministry.

Greater Opportunities

In 1980, BIMI built and dedicated a new building on Dodds Avenue in Chattanooga. It was a beautiful 10,000 square foot building on one acre of land. Dr. Freeny and the other staff believed it would be the largest building they would ever need. The day of the dedication was a wonderful time of rejoicing over God's unfolding work in world missions and through the work of BIMI.

It was also during this time that Pastor Sogoro Ogawa visited America. It was a breath of fresh air for the Sisks to finally have a friend from Japan visit the States. Don arranged for Pastor Ogawa to preach in many churches during his visit. He spoke English in many of them, and in others Don interpreted for him. It was a bit surreal, so many years later, to be interpreting in English for the preaching of his Japanese convert. Pastor Ogawa was inspired and encouraged by American Christians and was greatly used of God to help the American people see the need for missions in Japan.

In 1984, Dr. Freeny began making plans for his resignation. At this time, Don was spending considerable time during the summers in Asia. In fact, on four occasions he spent an entire summer on the island of Okinawa, filling in for missionaries on furlough and visiting various countries to encourage other missionaries. The Sisks had begun to pray about the possibility of purchasing a condominium or duplex in Chattanooga and renting something in Japan, which would allow them to spend half of their time in Japan, and the other half in America. This plan seemed perfect to them because of their frequent travel to Japan, but once again God was about to surprise them with other plans.

After returning to America in the late summer of 1984, several members of the Board of Directors of BIMI began contacting Don about an opportunity. Whether they had talked as a group was uncertain, but each one said the same thing: "Don, I believe you should be the next president and general director of BIMI."

At first, these unsolicited comments came as a complete shock to Don. Don had no aspirations for the position, and, besides that, Dr. Freeny had already chosen a successor under whom Don was thrilled to serve. The upcoming October board meeting was the determined time for the selection of Dr. Freeny's replacement. As the day drew closer, Don realized the board members were serious and he was indeed being considered for the position. All he could think was "Why me?" He felt completely inadequate on many levels, one of which was that BIMI was closely associated with Tennessee Temple University. Unlike many BIMI missionaries and board members, Don had not attended Tennessee Temple. This relieved him of thinking that the idea of his becoming the BIMI director was anything more than a remote possibility.

The only person Don discussed this possibility with was his son Tim, whom he asked to pray. A short time before the October board meeting, Don had a preaching engagement in Dallas and was able to spend a day with Tim, who was attending Dallas Theological Seminary. He told Tim, "I doubt this will happen, but if it does, I'm not sure I should accept it."

After a moment of prayer together, Tim said, "Dad, take it and go with it. If God is in it, you can do it." This was just what Don needed to hear in that moment. God had never failed him.

A Board Meeting that Changed Everything

The executive board meeting was held just a short time later. Don attended the meeting that evening with directors from various parts of the world. When it was time to discuss the new General Director, all of the field directors were asked to leave the room. After an hour of discussion, one of the men stepped into the room where the directors were waiting and announced that the board had unanimously voted to ask Don to become the new President and General Director of BIMI. Don sat still in his chair trying to absorb the news, but it seemed he was the only person that was surprised. All of the other field directors appeared confident about and in agreement with the decision. Don was simply shocked.

With gratitude, he accepted the position, telling the board members, "I will do the very best I can; however, I will not be in the office five days a week. I trust that God has led you in choosing me, but I know that God has called me to preach. Preaching in missions conferences will be my priority. I do not know much about office administration, but I know that God has called me to preach His Word and to stir the hearts of Christians for world evangelization."

The men agreed with his decision, knowing their greatest need as a missions organization was a man who would passionately represent BIMI and the cause of world missions in churches across America.

Don was in disbelief. And Virginia was at home with no idea of the news she was about to be given. It was about that moment that Don wondered if he should have mentioned it to her.

Seventeen

THE LORD SURPRISED

1984–1995

When Don left the BIMI board meeting that night, he returned home with Pastor Pat Creed, who was staying with the Sisks at the time. After greeting them, Virginia asked who had been selected as the new director. Don hadn't told Pastor Creed that Virginia had no idea he was being considered (a possibility that until that very night he had only thought remote), and before Don had a chance to answer her, Pastor Creed replied, "The new general director is Don."

Virginia laughed out loud, thinking this was a joke. When the men assured her it was true, Virginia began to cry. The responsibility of this new position—one that she had never considered a possibility—weighed heavily upon her heart. She slept very little that night, and kept asking Don, "How are we going to take on this new responsibility?"

It wasn't an unwillingness that brought her tears or stress; it was a feeling of inadequacy. The unknowns of their new responsibilities brought fear and hesitation. They were both willing, but neither one understood why God would ordain such a direction.

Growing into New Responsibilities

Don felt the weight of this unbelievable responsibility more than anyone else, but he also realized it was an unparalleled opportunity and the greatest open door God had ever shown him. He sought the prayers and counsel of every friend he knew.

Congratulatory messages poured in from across the world, but Don wasn't sure "congratulations" was the right word for his new, seemingly impossible situation. Of the many invaluable lessons God had taught him throughout the years, he knew that seemingly impossible situations were perfect opportunities for God to prove Himself strong. This was the case once again, as he began his role as the president of one of the largest mission organizations in the world.

In 1984, when Don began as general director, BIMI had about six hundred missionaries, a very tight budget, and pressing issues that needed immediate attention.

Don called a meeting with all of the organization's leaders. His predecessor, Dr. Tom Freeny, had been the first director of BIMI, and though the organization had grown and other leaders appointed, Dr. Freeny had made nearly all of the decisions in the organization and was familiar with every minute detail. In contrast, Don was new to many of the daily operational details. Most of his attention had been given to the Asian regions he served. He had no desire to the make final decisions on so many details. These and many other challenges early in his transition revealed that his new role was much broader in scope and influence than he'd been used to.

In that first meeting with other BIMI leaders, Don made it clear that his strongest leadership gifts were those of encouragement and delegation.

He told each of the field directors that what took place on their particular field was their responsibility, and the decisions they made would be the final decisions on those particular issues. He expected them to counsel with him concerning any major decisions, but once those decisions were made, he would not overrule them. And by the same token, he would not make a decision about any field or area of the ministry before consulting with them. In doing this, Don delegated not only the responsibility but also the authority to properly carry out the responsibility. This soon proved to be an effective method of leadership, and Don was able to immerse himself into learning the inner workings of BIMI.

Early on, he spent many hours with John Ramsey, BIMI's comptroller, working to understand the financial operation of the organization. The operational budget—the general fund from which the local office operated—was concerningly low. The organization was operating on a month-to-month basis, often coming dangerously close to not meeting its basic obligations. Don also felt that the retirement program was flawed and that the organization would be unable to fulfill in the long-term what had been promised to the missionaries. He immediately began working on a plan to rectify these problems.

Accepting a leadership position in any organization brings difficult decisions that must be made for long-term health. Not long into his tenure, Don was faced with just such a decision. BIMI had established a fully-functional printing ministry with a staffed print shop. Each month the ministry lost money because of its inability to maintain a work flow that covered the overhead costs.

Don determined to discontinue the printing ministry completely, using outside printers on an as-needed basis. This was a tough call because it meant some would lose their jobs, but it saved the organization money and alleviated the burden of needing to print for other churches. In the long term, it was the right decision.

Just Be You

Stepping into the new role gave Don a sense of fear and trepidation. He trusted God's providence, but he struggled with the "persona" of being the president of a prominent Christian organization. It was during this time that he happened to be preaching at a pastor's conference with Dr. Jack Hyles. He'd just listened to Dr. Hyles preach a sermon emphasizing the need to be anointed for every new ministry given by God, so he asked Dr. Hyles to pray with him for God's anointing and wisdom.

Before they prayed, Don told Dr. Hyles, "I have no idea how in the world I can do what I have been appointed to do." The other man responded, "Just be Don Sisk. Don't try to be Tom Freeny. Don't try to be anyone else. God knows you, and God knew who He was raising up for this position. Just be you."

This advice was a turning point for Don. He realized God had given him his personality and his new role, and the two were not incompatible. That conversation and moment of prayer gave Don the freedom to truly begin enjoying his new ministry.

A New Team and New Friends

One of Don's God-given strengths as a leader is building a team of qualified people who can excel in areas where he is weak. He had seen leaders in churches and other organizations who tended to hire according to their strengths, but Don determined to intentionally hire toward his weaknesses. Thus, over time, God allowed him to build a team with broad expertise in every area of missions work and the related technologies to support the organization. The BIMI team grew to be indispensable to their own ministry and to many other Christian organizations.

Don had met Dr. and Mrs. Ray Thompson in 1965. The Thompsons had gone directly to the mission field after graduating from college and had faithfully served for many years. The Sisks had cherished their long friendship with the Thompsons, and Don felt they would make a wonderful part of the BIMI team. The board of directors appointed Dr. Ray Thompson as the Executive Vice President of BIMI, and this was the beginning of a long, pleasant, and profitable partnership. Another team member Don depended upon heavily was Dr. Clifford Husky, the home director. In essence, Dr. Husky was the office manager, the secretary for the board of directors, and a liaison between the churches and the mission. Dr. Husky was a hard-working and diligent man of God, and a great member of the BIMI team.

During his first year in the directorship, God opened many doors for Don to preach and present the ministry of BIMI not only to local churches but also to fellowships, Bible colleges, seminaries, and conferences across the country. God gave him a wonderful working relationship with many Christian colleges. For many years, he spoke on a regular basis at Tennessee Temple University, Bob Jones University, Pensacola Christian College, Hyles-Anderson College, Trinity Baptist College, Crown College, West Coast Baptist College, Golden State Baptist College, and Ambassador Baptist College, as well as many other smaller institutions. These new relationships facilitated rapid growth for BIMI as many new missionaries went to the field from these meetings.

Honored for Service, Humbled in Leadership

God afforded Don many other responsibilities and honors with the leadership of BIMI. He was awarded honorary doctorate degrees from Faithway Baptist College in Ajax, Canada, Oklahoma Baptist College in Oklahoma City, Oklahoma, Trinity Baptist College in Jacksonville, Florida, and American Baptist College in Kokomo, Indiana. Each time he received an honor of this nature, he thought of the many people who had been used of God to bless his life and encourage him in the ministry.

In 1986 Don was elected as the moderator of the Southwide Baptist Fellowship. This was one of the most grueling years of his life in many ways, and serving to encourage cooperation amongst a broad group of people who define themselves as "independent" proved to be a challenging experience. In every setting, Don tried to promote unity rather than uniformity. He was thrilled to work together with so many different leaders toward the great task of worldwide evangelism.

Influencing the World

During his early years as director, Don placed an emphasis on field conferences—times when the missionaries of a particular region would gather to fellowship, hear the preaching of the Word of God, share testimonies, and receive personal encouragement for their families. This meant that Don not only traveled to Asia every year, but he began traveling and speaking in many other countries as well. He felt it was vital for the spiritual encouragement of BIMI missionaries that he and other speakers travel in person to their regions for conferences of encouragement and fellowship. He loved meeting with the missionaries of a given region, seeing what God was doing in their fields, and encouraging them on their own turf.

In practically every field conference, Don found missionaries in dire need of spiritual renewal and rest. It wasn't long before field conferences were established as an annual occurrence in every region of the world. Don and Virginia attended and spoke at many of these wonderful conferences. During these years, their influence for world missions grew in an immeasurable way. In the States, Don was speaking in conferences and on college campuses, where Christians were surrendering either to go or to give to missions. Then on foreign fields, Don was strengthening and equipping workers all over the world. Tens of thousands of people were growing in their love, labor, and generosity towards the ministry of the gospel because of Don's travels and influence.

Over a period of twenty years, through his ministry in field conferences, Don visited and ministered in more than sixty countries. Visiting missionaries gave him a working understanding of their lives, challenges, and potential. His extensive travel allowed him to have a broader and stronger impact for the gospel than he had ever imagined, but it also proved to be a challenging lifestyle to balance.

Memories of Traveling the World Together

As general director of BIMI, Don and Virginia had the opportunity to travel together. One of their favorite places to visit is Europe, and one year they were able to take a three-week trip to the continent. Two of the weeks were packed with meetings, but one week was free, and the Sisks used it to travel Europe.

Early that Monday morning they left Frankfurt and went to the Bavarian area of Germany where they shopped and discovered a new favorite food—apple strudel.

Later they visited the Dachau concentration camp where so many Jewish people were murdered during the Holocaust. They were devastated to see first hand where the horrific acts of the Holocaust had taken place. Don remembers, "To this day, those camps seem to have a cloud over them."

In Austria, they took the *Sound of Music* tour in Salzberg, staying in a little motel on the top of a mountain with breathtaking views for two beautiful days. The following day, their tour bus stopped near their motel where the guide explained that the field outside the bus was where the beginning of *Sound of Music* was filmed with Julie Andrews singing, "The hills are alive with the sound of music."

One night, they stayed in a little mountain town called Applestein. They felt they'd gone back two hundred years in history during their stay in this beautiful town with its many quaint shops. Early the next morning they were awakened by the ringing of church bells and saw a funeral procession heading through town with a casket being drawn by a horse and carriage.

All in all, it was an unforgettable trip. But it wasn't just the European sites that captivated the Sisks. While in Germany, they had the privilege of ministering in three military churches and four German-speaking churches. It was through these experiences that Don realized that Europe, particularly Western Europe, was one of the most difficult places in the world for evangelism. The trip made them even more appreciative of the courage of the missionaries ministering in these parts of the world.

Family Balance and Blessings

How does a man travel the world, minister to thousands of missionaries, facilitate the training of thousands of new missionaries, and still balance his personal life and marriage? Not easily. Don often found himself spread too thin as he tried to juggle his responsibilities through these years.

His administrative obligations were massive, and his travel schedule was heavy. He found himself constantly pulled in multiple directions and having to work harder to make time for things critical to his and his wife's spiritual well-being. This was a month-to-month battle, and he never felt that he consistently got it right. But together, he and Virginia tried to remain sensitive to and follow the leading of God's Spirit.

Renee Gets Married

After graduating from college, Renee went to the First Baptist Church of Hollywood, Florida, where she became a junior high school music teacher. God blessed her efforts there, and she was wonderfully used of Him. After several months, she began writing Don and Virginia about a young man named Tom Border who was the school band director. It wasn't long before Renee was engaged, and then a short time later, in the summer of 1975, Tom and Renee were married at the First Baptist Church of Hollywood, Florida. It was a beautiful wedding, and Don was proud that he was able to hold up rather well emotionally—until an unexpected moment in the ceremony. After Don prayed, Renee began singing a song inspired by the testimony of Ruth in Ruth 1:16, *"...whither thou goest, I will go; and where thou lodgest, I will lodge: thy people shall be my people, and thy God my God."* As Renee sang, Don was overwhelmed by the beautiful woman his little girl had become. Fortunately, the song lasted long enough that he was able to recover before his next part in the ceremony.

About two years later, Don and Virginia were pleasantly surprised when Renee told them they would be grandparents. On December 21, 1977, their first granddaughter, Rebecca Michelle, arrived, and the Sisks began to find themselves looking for any excuse to travel through Miami—even if they were heading from Chattanooga to Chicago. In what seemed like no time, Rebecca was playing the piano, singing, and delighting everyone that met her.

Another Wedding and an Empty Nest

Unlike his sister, Tim did not wait until after college to get married. At age sixteen, he'd met a young lady named Donna Chappell who captured his heart. Tim and Donna dated through high school and early college.

Once in college, he focused his energy on his education and his business, a cleaning service he had purchased. The business grew to provide enough income to sustain him, and shortly after his freshman year, Tim and Donna married.

Life brings with it many phases, and now many of them have names. For many years, children have grown, married, and left home—but now there's a name for it: the empty nest syndrome.

With their last child out of the home and beginning to start a family of his own, the Sisks began to experience the loneliness of an "empty nest." One night after Tim had gotten engaged, Don and Virginia were lying in bed when Virginia suddenly began to cry. She told him, "Renee's married and gone to Florida, and Tim and Donna are going to be married and they'll go to Dallas for seminary. Then we'll be all alone." He tried to encourage her by saying, "But honey, you still have me." As he remembers the story, "Then she *really* began to cry!"

Don thought that of the two of them, Virginia would have the harder time after Tim was married, but to his surprise, the change affected him more deeply than his wife. He would later say, "It's a rather humiliating time when the children are gone and no one is directly dependent on you; but when there are a lot of crying grandbabies around, I am often reminded that the empty nest syndrome is not so bad!"

With two married children, more grandchildren began to come along. A couple of years after Rebecca was born, Renee and Tom had a second beautiful daughter, Cassandra Ruth. And one evening, while on a trip to Mexico, Don received an unforgettable phone call from Tim informing him that he had a grandson: Donald Blake Sisk. The news was almost more than he could handle at the time. In the coming years, there would be three more grandchildren—Katie, Mallory, and Gabriel—born to Tim's family. God was just full of surprises!

Delighting in God's Surprise Blessings

One of the greatest delights to the Sisks was watching God lead their children to serve Him. Don and Virginia loved Japan and often wished they could be missionaries there again. In some ways they felt they had "sacrificed" their dream of returning. Little did they know how God would bring it back around through their children. As young families, both Tom and Renee and Tim and Donna were called of God to serve as missionaries to Japan. Soon Don and Virginia's two children were back on Japanese soil with their own children, ministering to old friends and reaching new ones. This was a blessing beyond measure to Don and Virginia, and it meant that annually the Sisks were able to return to Japan at Christmas. Before their trip, they would receive a long list of needs from their children and grandchildren and pack their clothing and personal items in carry-on bags so they could use their checked baggage to carry gifts and needed items.

These trips were restorative for Don and Virginia and were helpful to Tim and Renee, as well as to other missionaries on the field. Most astoundingly, these trips were the rebirth of long dormant dreams. God truly gave Don and Virginia the desires of their hearts in ways that only He could. Each year, they looked forward to their return to Japan and the wonderful family experiences that awaited them there.

Seasons of Delight

As Don and Virginia grew older, they found themselves drawing closer to one another and having more opportunities to be a blessing to a greater number of people. With no children in the home, Virginia was able to travel with Don more. This was a great blessing to the churches they visited, and, particularly, to the missionary families at the field conferences. Virginia was a great source of encouragement to young ladies and ministry wives, who appreciated her sharing her God-given wisdom. Although she was reluctant to speak publicly, her quiet spirit and her dedication to God made her a blessing to people all over the world.

During this season of life, God continually surprised and delighted Don and Virginia with unexpected blessings and opportunities. They could have never imagined all the ways God directed their path. In what seemed like a few years, their lives were greatly expanded. Together, the Sisks were leading a global missions organization, speaking around the world, influencing future missionaries, encouraging millions of dollars towards world missions, and cherishing their own children and grandchildren in Japan.

Following God and trusting Him often seems risky and sacrificial and can bring with it the fear of uncertain circumstances. But as the Sisks discovered, if we follow Him, we'll find the risk dissipates into the absolute security of God's guidance and presence, our sacrifices pale in comparison to God's blessings, and our fear gives way to the provision of God. To see and experience God's good heart, we must first choose to follow Him in faith. The heart of God to delight and surprise becomes wonderfully evident in retrospect. God is good, and while some times that's difficult to see when looking forward, it's impossible to miss looking backward.

Eighteen

THE LORD PROVIDED

1995–1996

One late September day, Don's secretary placed his mail on his desk at the BIMI home office. Among the pieces of junk mail, one brochure caught his eye. It was a large brochure entitled "Absolute Auction," and it described a 78.5-acre property on Harrison Bay, a beautiful place across from Harrison Bay State Park. On the property were a 40,000 square foot building, a house, and a multi-purpose building that had been used as a gymnasium and included a tennis court and a swimming pool. The minimum bid for the property was listed at $750,000, and it was obvious the property was worth several millions more. Don browsed through the brochure and dreamed of having the property for BIMI. The organization had already built a beautiful building on several acres outside of Chattanooga, but never could Don have imagined anything the size of the Harrison Bay property. And yet, for some reason, he just couldn't throw the brochure away.

The fact was that BIMI was in need of a new building. Under Don's leadership, BIMI had grown dramatically to over one thousand missionaries, and the home office had become much too small for the expanding ministry. For many months their property was listed in commercial property listings without any serious inquiries. In spite of its beauty and solid construction, it didn't appear that the property was marketable, primarily due to its location.

Some weeks later, on October 23 to be exact, Don suggested to Frank Rosser and Clifford Huskey that rather then going to lunch, they grab a sandwich to go and take a look at the Harrison Bay property together. Several people had encouraged Don to look into it, but knowing the value and BIMI's limited resources, he had not felt it was worth making the time. Carving a few minutes out during lunchtime seemed perfect.

After making some wrong turns, asking directions, and driving along Harrison Bay for some distance, the men eventually came to the entrance to the property, which had formerly been a drug rehabilitation center. As they entered, Don's heart began to race. It was one of the most beautiful places he had ever seen. And its main building so closely resembling the current BIMI building, with its white columns and similar brick construction, made Don speechless.

After walking the property and viewing its beauty, Don commented, "Humanly speaking there is absolutely no way we could get this. However there is a God in Heaven, and He does answer prayers."

In total faith, the three men knelt at the south end of the building and poured their hearts out to God: "God, this is what we need for the future expansion of BIMI. We do not have the means, but You own the cattle on a thousand hills, the hills, and all the wealth under the hills. Please give us this property."

Two days later, Don told BIMI's finance committee what he had seen and asked them to pray. After the meeting, Dr. Al Goss, Chairman of the Board of Trustees, went to see the property and was also impressed. Six days later, on October 31, Don went to bed but could not sleep. He got out of bed and went into his study to pray. During this time alone with God, the Lord gave him clarity on how to pursue this property.

Don Shares God's Plan

The next morning over breakfast, Don related to Virginia what God had shown him. If five hundred churches or individuals would make commitments of $1,000 each, they would raise $500,000 for the down payment and could bid up to a million dollars for the Harrison Bay property.

A short time later, after prayer time at the office, Don shared this vision with the office staff and asked them to pray as he called board members to ask them to consider this plan. He related it to as many of the field directors as he could and asked them to pray as well.

Later that week, Don called every pastor and Christian leader he could think of. He said the same thing to every one: "At Harrison Bay, just thirty minutes from our present property there is a 78 acre piece of property with a 40,000 square foot building along with some other buildings that could be used. I would like for you to pray with me about two things. I have decided after much prayer that if we could get $500,000 committed, we would bid up to a million dollars for the property. Please pray that the property will sell for less than a million dollars, which would be a miracle. Would you also pray about your church committing $1,000 for the property?"

That week Don was to preach at a missions conference in Winston-Salem, North Carolina. By Friday evening before the conference, over $90,000 dollars had been committed just from Don's phone calls.

A missionary to Albania by the name of Mike McCombie was sharing a room with Don that week, and after hearing Don's voice growing weak from so many phone calls, he offered to step in and make some calls as well. He had heard Don's speech so many times that he had it memorized. Don returned to Chattanooga on Monday, excited about what God was doing. He asked the field directors to be in the office as much as possible that week, and asked them all to call the pastors they knew, to pray, and to ask their missionaries to pray as well.

That week was one of the most exciting weeks Don had ever experienced in the ministry. Someone created a large chart to track progress, and every time a new commitment was obtained, it was posted to the chart. Each day that week, additional commitments came in as God worked in the hearts of more and more people.

People all over the world were praying about the fundraising effort and the upcoming auction. On Wednesday, Don drove to Greenville, North Carolina, for a conference with the People's Baptist Church and Pastor Max Barton. Many people urged him to return for the auction, but he didn't feel that was best. BIMI had contacted a professional to help them bid for the property, so Don really was not needed. Also, they had already decided not to bid anything over a million dollars. The board felt confident that they could sell their present property for approximately $400,000 and, with the commitments coming in, would be able to enter the new property nearly debt free.

All week, Don stayed in touch with the office regarding the progress of the commitments, which increased hourly. Every phone call Don made was positive. On Friday morning, one day before the auction, the total commitment was just over $500,000. Every leader, many missionaries, and hundreds of churches had made commitments. It was an amazing example of total cooperation on the part of independent Baptists around the world.

This Can't Be True, Can It?

The auction was scheduled for Saturday, November 11, at 10:00 AM. That Friday afternoon Don received a phone call from John Ramsey, who told him the Harrison Bay property had been sold and the auction canceled. Don was heart broken. Everything had seemed so positive; it was so apparent that God was going to give the property to BIMI. For about two hours Don wept and pleaded with God. He couldn't let go of the idea that this was God's will.

After two hours, the office was finally able to reach the people who were hosting the auction and learned that news of the sale was a false report. The auction was still scheduled as advertised. Don's relief was indescribable.

That night, the Peoples Baptist Church held a special time of prayer. All over the world people were praying that God would allow the auction to end in favor of BIMI.

Don had asked several men to attend the auction the next morning and to call him as soon as it was over. He waited patiently for the phone call from Ray Thompson.

We Got It!

Finally, at 11:30 the phone rang. Don's heart was racing, and his mouth was dry. What would the news be? Don picked up the phone and said, "Don Sisk."

Ray Thompson answered, "Doc, we got it!" Then he began to sob uncontrollably. Don wanted to know the final bid; he was fearful the men had bid beyond their limits. Ray replied that one party had bid the minimum $750,000 immediately. Then someone bid $775,000, someone else bid $800,000, and BIMI bid $805,000. Reluctantly, another bidder offered $810,000 and BIMI bid $815,000. No one else bid. Everyone was shocked that the bidding had stopped at such a low price.

BIMI was able to purchase the Harrison Bay property for a final bid of $815,000. Now it was Don's turn to weep, marveling at how God had answered prayer above and beyond what they had all asked.

A few days after the auction, the professional bidder BIMI had hired was in Don's office going over final details. To cap the story off, Don had the wonderful privilege of sharing the gospel with him and leading him to Christ. God had wonderfully worked in the entire situation.

Another Blessing From God

If BIMI had previously sold their property, they would have purchased land and built a far smaller facility. God had providentially placed a hold on selling the existing property. Within a few days of re-listing the current property, it was sold to an extended care nursing company for $445,000—more than Don expected to receive.

A multitude of work—planning, painting, carpeting, wiring, and much renovation—needed to be done before BIMI could occupy the Harrison Bay property. Following the auction and the sale of their existing property, a host of volunteers came together from BIMI's internal staff and churches all over the country who sent teams of laborers to help with the work. It was wonderful to see God send the right people at the right time.

One large group came from Messiah Baptist Church in Wichita, Kansas, and stayed for an entire week. They replaced the roof on the large building, completed much landscaping, and built a beautiful sign at the entrance of the property. In addition, the church family supplied most of the money for these projects.

EIGHTEEN—THE LORD PROVIDED

One of Don's great joys was to escort the Board of Trustees through the new property during the bi-annual meeting in December. Everyone was overjoyed to see what had been purchased and what was being done.

Through every detail, God provided enough money for the purchase as well as the remodel. It was miraculous to watch it all come together. Many gave, prayed, planned, and labored, and God gave the increase. In sixty years of ministry, Don says he has never seen a greater example of what God will do when His people work together with Him.

The Rest of the Story

In June of 1996 the BIMI "World Mission Center" was dedicated to God's glory. Over five hundred people were present during that week of celebration. Dr. Lee Roberson spoke at the dedication, reminding those in attendance of our need for compassion.

As of this writing, BIMI has occupied the Harrison Bay property for almost twenty years. Thousands have stayed in the twenty-five motel-style guest rooms that were beautifully furnished by individuals and churches. Camp BIMI has been hosted annually, and hundreds of young people from many countries have attended camp and developed a heart for world missions. Many of these teens are now serving as missionaries with BIMI. Hundreds of missionaries have candidated and been prepared from this place and are now serving around the world.

The property is also home to retired missionaries who live onsite and assist in the World Mission Center work of preparing new missionaries as well as forming a prayer team for worldwide evangelization.

Houses have been built on the property for staff and for missionaries on deputation and furlough. Workshops and storage buildings have been erected. Hundreds of workers from many churches have assisted in the construction of these buildings. God has allowed BIMI to serve many groups and missions organizations because of the Harrison Bay property.

Don's prayer is that God will use the property for His glory until the Lord Jesus returns.

To this day, Don never drives into the entrance of the World Mission Center without thanking the Lord for what He has done…and anticipating so much more that He will yet do!

Nineteen

THE LORD REDIRECTED

1996–2006

For more than forty years, Don Sisk traveled somewhere every week to influence people for world missions. (He often tells people that he feels like a drug addict because he's always "on a trip.")

Having spent so much time in Baptist churches, he has met many people in the ministry who feel underpaid, underappreciated, and underutilized in their positions. These people are miserable and their joy is gone. But their loss of joy is not a casualty of serving God; it's a casualty of a bad attitude.

As Don has observed, although the Apostle Paul was rarely appreciated, rarely paid, and spent a good portion of his life serving in ways well below his education and ability, he never got over the fact that God allowed him to be in the ministry. Even in the latter years of his life, he was amazed that God would count him faithful and allow him to serve

Jesus Christ with his life. When it comes to ministry, God knows exactly what He's doing. We who serve Jesus Christ ought to be thankful that God allows us to do so in spite of who we really are. God does not choose us *because* of who we are, but *in spite* of who we are, so He can make us who we ought to be for His glory.

Stepping Down from BIMI

In June of 2002, at the age of seventy, Don resigned his position as President and General Director of Baptist International Missions, Inc. He had served faithfully, joyfully, and energetically in the position for eighteen years, and God used him to impact the entire world for Jesus Christ.

Though he knew God was leading him to resign, Don's resignation was no retirement; he knew God had more for him to do. Don had never "sat still" in ministry, and traditional retirement held no attraction for him. He has chosen to press forward as long as God gives him energy and opportunity, staying active and involved in the ministry of the gospel.

And yet, what Don *was* surprised with was what—and where—this would look like.

Invitation to the Desert

God placed a desire in Don's heart to work with and spend time developing young leaders and future missionaries. With whatever time and ability God gave, Don decided he would invest into the future of the gospel flowing from independent Baptist churches.

Don continued a full travel schedule, which in the summer of 2002 included preaching at the Spiritual Leadership Conference in Lancaster, California, hosted by Dr. Paul Chappell, pastor of Lancaster Baptist Church and president of West Coast Baptist College.

NINETEEN—THE LORD REDIRECTED

Dr. Sisk was no stranger to Lancaster Baptist. In fact, he shared a close friendship with Pastor Chappell forged one surprising, providential moment at a preacher's conference fifteen years previous. He had been visiting with a pastor and slipped in late one session to a back row seat. He greeted the man already seated in the row with his usual cheerfulness and warmth, and he offered him a copy of his book, *Joyful Giving*.

What he didn't know was that the pastor in the seat next to him—also attending the conference as a speaker—was pastoring a rapidly growing church in the high desert of Southern California, had a fervent heart for missions, was experiencing growing pains at the church…and was in need of a friend.

In the next few moments, God—as only He can do—knit the two men's hearts into what has become a close friendship and mentorship that has spanned almost a quarter of a century.

So when Don flew out to Lancaster in July of 2002 to preach at Spiritual Leadership Conference, he was looking forward to seeing and fellowshipping with Pastor Chappell again. What he wasn't expecting was the invitation Pastor Chappell had been praying about extending to him—teaching missions during the spring semester at West Coast Baptist College.

There were so many unexpected elements to this request: Don had originally planned to home-base from Chattanooga (a verdant Garden of Eden compared to the high desert of Lancaster). He had looked forward to being near the familiar surroundings of Chattanooga and hosting pastors who came to visit BIMI.

And yet, to Don and Virginia's surprise, as they prayed and talked about this opportunity, they both began to sense God's leading. After all, it was just a request for one semester. And, it fit perfectly with the burden God had placed on Don's heart to invest in future independent Baptist missionaries. After many years of ministry transitions, God was redirecting the Sisks once again, this time to Lancaster, California, for yet another chapter of ministry adventures.

Why Would You Move Again?

Many people asked the Sisks, "Why would you pack up and go to a place like Lancaster in your retirement years?" Looking back, Don believes it's probably one of the best decisions they ever made. What began as a commitment to "teach one semester" has turned into over a decade of investing the spring semester every year into future missionaries, pastors, and servant leaders as an instructor and the head of the college's missions department. Fruit continues to abound to Don and Virginia's account through the scores of West Coast Baptist College graduates serving as missionaries on foreign fields around the world.

But how does a couple with the age and experience of the Sisks come to such a decision late in life? For that matter, how did they arrive at each of their decisions to relocate over the course of their married lives?

Don gets asked these questions, and he begins by explaining four factors that have *not* led them to accept new opportunities:

They never moved for physical conditions—Don believes that Christian leaders should never choose where to live and where to serve simply because of physical reasons. Geographic changes don't change who we are. Contentment is an internal decision, not an external condition. The problems of life never improve simply because of a new location.

To illustrate that we ought to be content where and with whom God places us, Don tells a story about a man traveling on an airplane who noticed that the man next to him was wearing his wedding ring on the wrong hand. After a few moments his curiosity got the best of him and he asked the man, "Excuse me, but aren't you wearing your wedding ring on the wrong hand?" The other man answered, "Yes…I married the wrong woman." If we aren't careful, we too will decide we are with the wrong people, and we'll face great discontentment.

They never moved for financial benefits—In sixty years of ministry, the Sisks never allowed financial compensation to determine where they would serve God or how they served. Don learned long ago that if we take care of God's business, He will take care of ours.

They never moved for family connections—Although Don and Virginia believe that family is a God-given priority and although they miss their children and grandchildren, they don't believe avoiding physical separation from family should keep us from being where God wants us to be. As Don wisely observes, "If everybody had to stay close to extended family all the time, we would have no missionaries."

They never moved for lack of opportunities—When Don prepared to retire, he had many ideas of what he might do. He thought about preaching missions conferences full time. He considered visiting foreign countries as a full-time minister to missionaries. He considered full-time writing or teaching at various schools and educational institutions. Frankly, he could have joined a country club and played golf five days a week.

But the Sisks moved across the country because they clearly believed God was directing them to join in the work of training future missionaries with Pastor Chappell and the team of educators at West Coast Baptist College. They believed God had opened yet another door of ministry to them, and they wanted to obey Him and seize the moment for His glory.

In hindsight, it is easy to see the impact this choice has had. Today, there are missionaries all over the world, with more graduating into the harvest fields each year, who sat at the feet of Don and Virginia Sisk in missions classes at West Coast Baptist College. The Lord has used the Sisks' years at the college to further the work of missions and multiply their ministry to a greater magnitude than they ever dreamed. In addition to teaching in the college, Don has helped numerous churches on the

West Coast, counseled hundreds of West Coast Baptist College students, and encouraged and mentored many of God's servants.

God used a vision to speak to the Apostle Paul and lead Him to Macedonia. If Paul were asked why he went, he would have simply said, "God led me to go." Over the centuries, God has chosen different methods to call and direct His people, but He has never failed to lead them. As they continue to follow God through faith, the Sisks know that wherever they are, the reason they are there and doing what they are doing for God is simply because He put them there.

Providential Placement

Little did Don realize how truly providential his placement in Lancaster would be, especially for Virginia's health. At the time of their relocation, Virginia's growing brain tumor was a few years from being large enough to be detected, but God strategically placed them in Southern California for this looming trial.

By His remarkable grace, He had prepared one of the nation's premier neurosurgeons to operate on Virginia at Don's most trying hour of life. That surgeon "happened" to work at Cedars-Sinai Hospital in Los Angeles, and one of his staff "happened" to be a faithful member at Lancaster Baptist Church.

God was ordering steps far ahead of Don and Virginia and making the crooked places straight, as He always does. Just on the horizon, right after a delightful ministry cruise to Alaska, was some terrifying news, a series of tests, a high-risk brain surgery…

…and the most grueling two-hour wait that Don had ever endured.

Twenty

THE LORD PRESERVED

2006

Don's remembrances grew deeper and the waiting room quieter as the clock ticked agonizingly slow seconds away. It had been four hours since he had stood by Virginia's side and prayed with her, and two hours since the surgery began. Several times during those waiting hours, the family and friends with Don had gathered around him to pray for the surgeons and nurses and for Virginia. Through it all, Don was pondering things that couldn't properly be expressed in mere words.

His heart dropped and a lump formed in his throat as Dr. Hunt, one of Virginia's surgeons, entered the waiting room. It was 11:00 AM, just as expected, but waiting for an update from the doctor had been the most traumatic and excruciating experience Don could recall. Don braced himself to hear news that would change the remainder of his life as questions raced through his mind. Did Virginia survive? Was there brain damage? Was the tumor cancerous? Was it removed or would it continue to grow?

Dr. Hunt spoke methodically, "Mr. Sisk, the surgery was successful. We were able to remove all of your wife's tumor. The tumor was benign, and we were able to remove it without doing any damage to your wife's brain. We believe she'll make a full recovery."

Tears of joy welled up in Don's eyes, and sighs of relief echoed around the waiting room. As the doctor excused himself, the group gathered, bowed their heads, and, with great relief and rejoicing, thanked God for answering their requests. Don's heart swelled with gratitude to God for preserving his faithful companion and allowing them to enjoy more time to serve their Saviour together.

The Recovery Room

An hour later, Don was sitting by Virginia's recovery room bedside as she began to regain consciousness. As she came to, she smiled and told Don, "I kept thinking all along about the song 'What a Mighty God We Serve.'"

Don shared with her the good news the surgeon had given them, and shortly after Virginia was taken to a room in the ICU and enjoyed a restful night. Cards, flowers, phone calls, and email messages were still pouring in from praying friends around the world. The Sisks' faith was strengthened. They felt closer to one another and a greater love for one another and for the Lord.

On Saturday morning, Virginia was transferred to a regular room, and the Sisks continued to be cared for by the skilled staff at Cedars-Sinai, as well as by family and friends that continued to express love and prayers. Virginia was amazed at the outpouring of love and just kept saying to Don, "We aren't worthy of all this care!"

That night Don asked for a cot so he could stay the night in the room with his wife. This wonderful lady had cared for him for nearly sixty years, and he considered it a privilege to care for her through this time.

Going Home Early

Monday was a trying day of emotional ups and downs; it brought with it a flurry of doctors and therapists, all with varying opinions on how long Virginia's hospital stay would be and how difficult her recovery would be. When Dr. Hunt came to visit, he was pleased with her recovery and expressed that most of her therapy could be done at home. She would be released the next morning, and Don and Renee would be responsible for helping with her therapy and recovery from home.

Don asked the doctor if there were any special rules to follow for her recovery to which Dr. Hunt replied, "If it hurts, don't. If it doesn't hurt, do." He advised that it would take some time for Virginia's memory to recover fully and for her full mental faculties to return.

By noon the next day, Tuesday, Don, Virginia, and Renee were exiting the hospital parking lot to return home. As they arrived home at 2:30 that afternoon, they found the front door covered with welcome home signs—expressions of love from members of Lancaster Baptist Church and students of West Coast Baptist College. The long journey toward recovery had begun with an encouraging boost.

The Journey Ahead

Although recovery took time, the Sisks were grateful for the opportunity to be together and thankful that Virginia was progressing faster than expected. Daily, she made progress in her walking, thinking, and spirit. Daily they continued to sing, "This Is the Day the Lord Hath Made."

Don canceled scheduled meetings that week and limited the number of visitors that could come to the house so he, Virginia, and Renee could spend time together and focus on Virginia's recovery.

The following paragraphs are excerpts taken directly from Don's journal during Virginia's recovery time at home. It picks up that first week that Virginia was home and gives insight into their relationship and attitude toward this time of trial:

"We limited the number of visitors that could come to the house. We enjoyed fun times together. We prayed much, and many times each day thanked God for His goodness. Phone calls, emails, flowers, and fruit treats continued to come, as well as gifts of various kinds. Saturday I left the house only for a few minutes to go to the grocery store and to get other necessary things for the house. I watched a lot of football. Was very pleased that University of Kentucky beat Louisville. What a game. I also watched some golf."

"On Sunday I attended the early service…Later that evening, Dr. Chappell and several others left after church to begin their trip to the Philippines, Korea, and China. I was scheduled to go with them. I am so happy that I can stay here with Virginia. It is a blessing to serve her."

"Monday morning I arose early and took a long walk, did some work in the yard, and had some wonderful time in the Bible before Virginia or Renee awoke. It was good that they could get some much-needed rest. We took Virginia outside for a walk for the first time today."

"I called today to cancel my meeting with Temple Baptist Church in Flower Mound, Texas, pastored by one of my best friends, Dr. Richard Wallace. I had been at that church twenty-eight years in a row for their conference. We are living life one day at a time. Thank Him for each day. In the afternoon the physical therapist came for about an hour. He gave us a series of exercises that she could do twice daily. It has been a good day. Our friends, Leo and Evelyn, are coming to the house after they serve at the school."

"It was a wonderful week together. Daily we rejoiced as Virginia gained strength and memory. She exercised and progressed much quicker than one could have hoped."

"Thank God Renee had been able to stay with us for a month. Her help to us was remarkable, but it was a sad goodbye. I do not know how we would have done without her. It was a very sad day for us."

"Daily we continue to sing 'This is the day the Lord hath made, we will rejoice and be glad in it.' Daily she continues to make great progress."

"On the first of October, we went to the medical center for her post-operation appointment. Again it was a very positive time. Dr. Hunt expressed that everything had gone well and that there would be no need to see him for a year. At that time she will have another MRI. However he expressed his belief that the tumor would not return. And stated that if it should start to grow back (only a 1% chance), it would be removed by radiation without surgery."

"Virginia is now functioning at her normal pace. She continues to exercise, get some rest in the afternoons, and get to bed as early as possible. Praise God for grace and mercy during this great trial. We would not have chosen it, but it has made us better and certainly more appreciative."

"God has been so real to us during this. He has provided our every need. The Lord hath done great things for us and we are glad."

"It has now been nine months since the operation, and Virginia continues to function well. There have been no adverse effects from the operation. In fact she is doing much better than she has in years. We have been able to minister to several people because of this experience. I have testified to many about the wonderful, miraculous working of God."

Just a few months after her operation, Virginia had a severe cold, so Don took her to the doctor. Her primary care physician had been given a negative report on her condition, so he was expecting her to be far worse than she was. When he stepped into the waiting room and saw her sitting in a chair, looking well, he pointed at her and said to those in the room, "Folks, sitting right here is a miracle of God!"

Don smiled, squeezed Virginia's hand, and thought, "Praise God! He gets all the glory, and I get to keep my wife!"

Conclusion

THE LORD LED

2006–2015

What a story. What an incredible tapestry of wonder God weaves in such a short vapor. What a beautiful story He writes in the lives of those who trust Him in faith.

And the story isn't complete. At eighty-two years of life, Don is celebrating sixty years in the ministry—*sixty years* of walking with God, following His leading, preaching the gospel, leading the lost to Christ, challenging churches to obey the Great Commission, and now reaping the fruit of six decades in ministry.

Taking It All In

In late August 2014, Dr. Sisk preached to the church family at Emmanuel Baptist Church in Newington, Connecticut. During this trip, he and I spent a number of hours working on this manuscript. As always, we laughed a lot. (Nobody has more funny one-liners than Don Sisk.)

We reflected on his decades of marriage and ministry and discussed life lessons that emerged through the years:

Worry Less—In over eighty years of life, Don has learned that worry is less fruitful than we think. He said, "If I was doing it all over again I probably wouldn't worry at all." Then he paused and amended, "On second thought, maybe worrying did some good, because hardly anything I ever worried about actually happened." Truly, in eternity we will all look back on our lives and regret that we ever worried at all.

More Family Time—Don is so grateful that his children serve the Lord and have continued to faithfully honor Jesus. Reflecting upon their early family life and ministry, he said, "If I was doing it all over again I would spend a lot more time with my children." Good advice from a faithful man.

Laugh a Lot—Don Sisk exudes the joy of the Lord, in spite of the trials of life. He laughs more than anyone most people have ever met; in fact, hanging out with him for awhile is reminiscent for me of being around teenagers in youth ministry—laughter abounds. Don Sisk has learned the skill of taking the ministry very seriously, but taking himself very lightly. He allows Jesus Christ to increase and himself to decrease.

Keep Working on Marriage—After sixty-two years with Virginia, Don has learned that marriage is something that must be worked on daily during a couple's entire life together. There is no such thing as a utopian marital plateau.

Age with Joy—Being around Don gives one a sense of hope that aging doesn't have to be depressing. Joy is an intentional choice, and it's contagious. Discontentment may be defined in part as being in one season of life, but wishing to be in another. Don Sisk has embraced every season of life with delight, rejecting the temptation to look too far back or ahead. He lives in this moment, grateful for it, and refuses to grow melancholy about past or future seasons.

Keep Learning—At a time when many others his age struggle to use a cell phone, Don is proficient with his smart phone, computer, and iPad. He has a large ebook library and continues to read, learn, pursue God, and grow in grace as if he were just getting started. He refuses to stagnate or grow lethargic. He may have aged, but he's definitely not old!

Avoid Ego Traps—In his decades of ministry Don has not only met but had the privilege to know many great people and leaders in Christendom who are now in Heaven—men like Tom Malone, Lee Roberson, Bob Jones, Jerry Falwell, Adrian Rogers, John R. Rice, and literally hundreds of other servants of God. When asked why there have been so many problems and politics clouding issues between Christians who believe nearly exactly the same thing, he gives one simple answer: "Ego." He's right.

Avoid the Nonsense—Don has locked in on the advancement of the gospel and the evangelization of the world by remaining focused on big battles and refusing to be drawn into petty arguments, divisive thinking, and polarization. He has followed Jesus' command and Paul's example to avoid comparison or competition between personalities and to appreciate anyone who preaches the gospel of Christ even if he may not be able to directly work with him.

Be Humble—Over the years Don has spoken at many major Bible training institutions and has been awarded eight honorary doctorates. (I tease him that he is an "honorary doctorate hog.") This man has more honors and ministry achievements than he can remember, and yet he laughs it all off with a grateful and humble heart.

Love Everybody—Those who have spent much time with Dr. Sisk will realize they've never heard him speak ill of others and never known him to harbor anger, bitterness, or ill-will toward anyone. He does not despise or fight with other Christians. He just loves and encourages people.

No Generation Gap—One thing Don has noticed while working with others in various ministries is that many younger men have no interest in having a relationship with older men who have been where they are and are still desiring to serve God. These younger men see age as a hindrance rather than a treasure of experience, wisdom, and grace. There should be no generation gap in the ministry, and Don Sisk makes this easy. He's neither proud nor judgmental, but is genuinely loving, encouraging, joyful, and wise. Perhaps his story will compel you to close the generation gap and tap into the hearts of men like him. They have much to contribute to our lives as we press on together for Jesus.

Finish Strong—Despite all that he has accomplished in faith during his life, Don keeps going. He keeps preaching the same gospel he began preaching over sixty years ago. He never lost interest in seeing people come to Jesus Christ and in personally telling others about the grace of God.

The Lord Led

At eighty-two years of age, Don Sisk has had an amazing life and it's not over yet. His health is solid and his mind is strong, and he's still preaching all over America, many times in the company of his wife. Every spring, the Sisks spend a semester at West Coast Baptist College in Lancaster, California, helping prepare young adults for a life in service of the gospel. The rest of the year, the Sisks can be found in their home on the Harrison Bay property, the headquarters of BIMI—where Don still has an office. From the Chattanooga area, he still travels the country and often to foreign fields preaching God's Word and challenging others to invest their lives and resources into world evangelization.

In 3 John 4, the Apostle John wrote, "*I have no greater joy than to hear that my children walk in truth.*" Don and Virginia rejoice that God has blessed their two children, six grandchildren, and four great-grandchildren and used them in His work over the years. Renee and Tim have been active in world evangelization all of their adult lives. Both served in Japan as missionaries, and Tim also served in Bolivia. After fourteen years in Japan, Tom and Renee are now involved in a ministry reaching Japanese in the Dayton-Cincinnati, Ohio, region. Tim is chairman of the Missions Department of Moody Bible Institute and also pastors a church.

The Sisks' "spiritual children" are also doing well. Hardly a day passes that they do not get a phone call, email, text, or other communication from someone whose life was impacted by their ministry, and Don and Virginia praise God with joy for these testimonies of God's faithfulness.

Today there are thousands of servants of God faithfully laboring on foreign fields and tens of thousands who have been brought to Jesus Christ as a direct or indirect result of the Sisks' ministry. Hundreds of millions of dollars have been sent to foreign fields as a result of Don's preaching on stewardship and the joy of giving.

Don and Virginia are more in love and closer to each other than ever. They believe their last decade together has been a gift from God, and they have cherished every day since Virginia's surgery in 2006. Several years later, her tumor returned, to their great concern, and this time was not resolvable by radiation. Virginia underwent a second surgery, from which she recovered fully, and follow-up radiation to prevent the tumor from returning. In late 2014, the tumor again returned, and Virginia is once again undergoing radiation, undergirded with prayers from around the world.

Don has written several books over the years, and his most recent, *The Fourth Quarter*, came out of Don's experience of being led by God into his most fruitful and spiritually productive season of life just when he thought his ministry was slowing down. He challenges readers who are entering their retirement years to redeem their fourth quarter of life for God's glory. And they have a wonderful example to look to. Don Sisk is still pressing on for the Lord. Wherever his finish line is, he intends to run across it with all of his might, by God's grace and for His glory.

When Don looks back on his life, he laughs. To him it still seems unbelievable that God would choose to work through him, and he rejoices in all that God has allowed him to see, do, and be part of. And of the more than sixty-five years of being a Christian, sixty-two years of marriage to Virginia, sixty years of ministry, and fifty years in full-time missions, he would not change a single day—because God did it all.

...I being in the way, the Lord *led me...*—Genesis 24:27

Acknowledgements

This story has been eighty-two years in the making, and it's still being written. This book has been roughly eight years in process.

Several months prior the completion of this manuscript, I had the opportunity to spend a few days with Dr. Sisk. I had missed him! When in California, our offices were directly adjacent to each other, and I had forgotten how much I missed "hanging out" with Dr. Sisk. We talked, visited, and shared laughs often during those years.

Few people have had as profound an impact on my life as this godly man. I was honored beyond words when he invited me into the process of writing his story. This project has been a life-changing challenge. Understanding and telling Don Sisk's story has been, for me, an unforgettable journey of personal growth. His life and heart have left an indelible mark on my soul. Throughout this process, I often had to pause, dry my tears, and catch my breath before I could resume writing.

Thank you, Dr. Sisk, for living the dream and then sharing it with us. Thank you for allowing me to be a part of crafting the narrative, and thank you for being patient with me over several years of unpredictable circumstances that lengthened this project's timeline considerably.

Thank you to my wife and family for patiently encouraging and tolerating the process of writing a book. Putting up with the consumed mind of an author requires a special grace!

Thank you, Melanie Anderson, for your typing of Dr. Sisk's many hours of original dictation. You were the first crucial part of a lengthy process, and I am grateful for your incredible help.

Thank you, Sonia Birdsong, for your writing assistance in working with a very rough, original draft. Your long hours provided a strong foundation upon which to build. I am grateful for your dedicated hours and hard work.

Thank you to those early editors and readers who invested time and focus into making this a more readable, engaging story. Your skills invested in this project made it a better testimony to a great life and a great God.

Thank you, Pastor Chappell and the team at Striving Together Publications, for bringing this project into its final form and for making it available for many to benefit from Don and Virginia Sisk's journey of faith.

ABOUT THE AUTHOR

CARY SCHMIDT is the senior pastor of Emmanuel Baptist Church of Newington, Connecticut. He and his wife, Dana, have been married twenty-five years and have three children—Lance (married to Hillarie), Larry, and Haylee—and two twin grandchildren—Chad and Charleigh. Cary is a gifted communicator who is passionate to share God's truth.

Also available from
Striving Together Publications

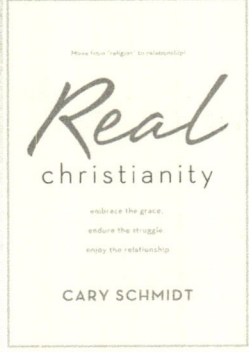

Real Christianity
In this compelling book, Cary Schmidt candidly and simply unpacks what real Christianity is all about. Through these pages, learn how you can embrace the grace, endure the struggle, and enjoy the relationship of truly knowing Jesus! This book will revitalize your walk with the Lord, and you will want to purchase a copy for everyone you know.
(240 pages, paperback)

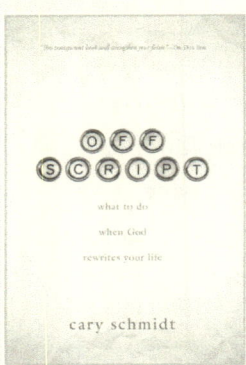

Off Script
Every now and then, God takes our lives off script. He reaches into our circumstances with events we would never choose. If your world has gone awry, if your life is off script, this book will help you discover God's heart, joy, and truth in the fog of an uncertain reality.
(240 pages, hardback)

Passionate Parenting
This book allows an up-close look to see how children are ruining their lives and how their parents are helping them do it! This book is uniquely written to young people and their parents. It helps kids understand where their parents are coming from and helps parents understand how to help their children by "standing in the gap" before it is too late.
(288 pages, paperback)

strivingtogether.com

Also available from Striving Together Publications

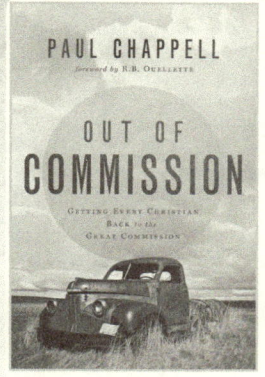

Out of Commission
Written for every Christian who desires to obey the Great Commission of Christ, this comprehensive volume is motivational and practical, diagnostic and corrective. Whether you are new to evangelism or an experienced soulwinner, *Out of Commission* will challenge and equip you to share your faith and more effectively reach your community for Christ. (256 pages, hardback)

Stewarding Life
God has given you one life and filled it with resources—time, health, finances, relationships, influence, and more. How you steward these resources will determine whether you successfully fulfill God's eternal purpose for your life. This book will take you on a personal stewardship journey, equipping you to live effectively and biblically. It will challenge and equip you to strategically invest your most valuable resources for God's eternal purposes. (280 pages, hardback)

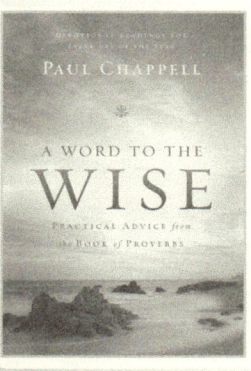

A Word to the Wise
In this power-packed daily devotional, each page shares a nugget of wisdom from the book of Proverbs. Written for the practically-minded Christian, each reading concludes with a distilled truth that you can immediately apply to your life. Let God's wisdom from the book of Proverbs equip you for the challenges of your daily life. (424 pages, hardback)

strivingtogether.com

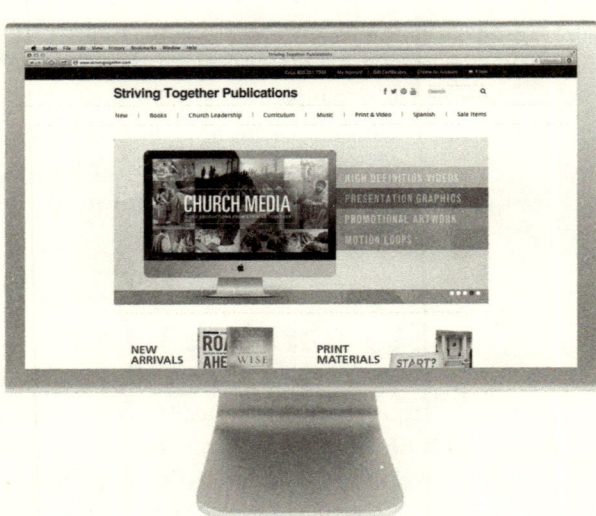

Visit us online

strivingtogether.com

wcbc.edu